A P

# A Place in the Mind
## – a Boyhood in Llŷn

R. Gerallt Jones

gomer

First impression – 2004

ISBN 1 84323 365 7



This book is published with the financial support of the Welsh Books Council.

*Printed in Wales at*
*Gomer Press, Llandysul, Ceredigion SA44 4QL*

*I Wlad Llŷn:*
*yno y gorwedd gwreiddiau'r cyfan*

# Foreword

This was a long labour, a labour of love, of intense love. I think it may have taken Gerallt almost a decade to write this book, to ponder over it and analyse it, packed between other works. And this was one script that he was most anxious to have published. During Gerallt's years as Warden of Gregynog, the children having completed their educational careers in various universities, we had the luxury of spending about four consecutive annual holidays, in September, in Llŷn, and it was in these breaks that the enchantment of Llŷn fell upon him again. During the last war, he said, all signposts were removed, so as to add to the confusion of the enemy. The result was that he knew the map of Llŷn utterly, totally, and the network was unchanged. He was thus able to wander freely, able to dream of finding Llŷn again as a place of wonder and magic and mysticism and odd reality. He expressed a wistful wish to retire there, a wish never fulfilled. He died in January 1999.

Sŵ Gerallt Jones

# I

For me, born and bred within its boundaries, Llŷn was always a very clearly-defined locality. It had firm, rational frontiers, which made it, in effect, not a peninsula but an island, a circumscribed world of its own. On the southern side, Llŷn stopped at Pwllheli, for Pwllheli was the railhead, and it was from Pwllheli that the railway train eventually took me away to school, to the hostile world where Welsh was no longer an acceptable linguistic currency. On the northern side, Llŷn came to an end when the road leading from Nefyn to Caernarfon climbed over the shoulder of Yr Eifl and descended to the alien village of Llanaelhaearn and the country beyond. Subjective though such a definition might be, it is the one I shall adopt, for it enclosed my childhood environment. It is the place that remains for ever in the mind.

In my childhood – during the late 30s and 40s – Llŷn was still an entity in itself. It was, of course, the end of an era. The war was to change everything. It would never again be commonplace to find people, however elderly, who had never travelled beyond Pwllheli. It would never again be possible for a child, growing up at the foot of Garn Fadryn, to experience an environment where

Welsh was the natural medium of all communication, and to suppose that all those human beings who did not speak Welsh were, by definition, English; non-Welsh-speaking Welshmen did not exist. The boundaries of a locality of perhaps sixty square miles would no longer be regarded as an adequate world within which people could, with reasonable contentment, live out their lives.

This is to idealise the situation. There was great poverty, there was much unhealthy in-breeding, there was parochialism and ignorance. But a child's world is an ideal world, and for a child it was enough. It may be too that such a world retained within it certain childlike qualities that the world outside had lost.

And so to begin with Pwllheli. It is, in fact, by one of those ironies that proliferate in Llŷn, an ancient Norman borough. This is how Thomas Pennant recounted its beginnings in his *Tour of North Wales*, published in 1810:

> It lies close to the shore, and has a tolerable harbour for vessels of about sixty tons. The entrance is by a high rock called the Gimlet, a mile from land, to which it is joined by a range of sand-hills. This place was made a free borough by the Black Prince, by charter, dated the 12th year of his principality, at Caernarfon . . .

The charter was granted to a local Norman landowner, Nigel de Lohareyn, who was one of the gentlemen of the Prince's bedchamber; the burgesses of Pwllheli were consequently to pay the landowner £14 a year for their privileges, which included the considerable benefits of organizing their own trading arrangements under licence.

And it is of trading arrangements that we first think when Pwllheli comes to mind nowadays. Whether you enter the town by road or rail, you come to an open square, with the railway station on the one hand, a row of shops on the other. From the square, a road, straight as a die, leads to the sea, passing the deserted harbour as it goes. On the sea-front itself, there is nothing but the wind blowing up from the south-west, and a forlorn row of weather-beaten guest-houses. There is a promenade, but it leads inconclusively to a road which runs parallel to the one along which you came. Turning down this, past the recently-built comprehensive school, you return to a second open square, Y Maes, which is the hub of Pwllheli's existence. From it, the buses make their way in and out of Llŷn.

Before turning to the fair, and to the real life of 'Y Dref' (for Pwllheli, to the inhabitants of Llŷn, is simply 'The Town'), it is necessary to explain the sense of barren futility that greets one on one's diverted journey to the sea and back, the peculiar unfinished pathos of West End and South Beach. The name Pwllheli means 'salt pool' and most of the land the town now stands on was originally washed by the tides before the row of sand-hills described by Pennant created a natural breakwater for the cluster of houses around the shore. When Nigel de Lohareyn received his reward for his deeds in France, he may well have been dismayed with his present, for no one had ever bothered to build town walls to protect the burgesses, or a castle to provide a focus of attention. From the start, Pwllheli was allowed to remain a local centre, and succeeded in remaining at least partially Welsh. Its very nonentity prevented it from becoming Normanised and Anglicised. It was not important enough to be developed.

But as time went on, it spread itself modestly behind its barricade of sand, and grew to be a fishing port, and later a location for the building of sailing-ships, while still fulfilling its genuine function as a market town for the peninsula. During the latter half of the nineteenth century, however, as sedate and seemly Victorian tourism gently invaded the coasts of Britain, the considerable potential of Pwllheli's scenic views of Eryri and the coast did not go unnoticed. In a jolly guidebook produced by the Great Western Railway in 1911 under the title, *North Wales – the British Tyrol*, the whole issue was comprehensively summed up in this way:

> Pwllheli is so richly endowed by nature, both as regards scenery and climate, that it is rapidly realising the expectations of its most sanguine admirers, as one of the most rising watering-places of this portion of the Welsh littoral . . . No less a sum than between £60,000 and £70,000 is being spent on the conversion of the existing tidal basin into a deep water harbour, and quite within recent years local enterprise, mainly represented by Mr S. Andrews and his son, has brought into existence both the West End Parade and the tramways. Substantial contributions to the necessary cost

> were made both by the Government and the Cambrian Railways, the latter bringing their line into town . . .

A lady tourist, writing to the *Gentlewoman* magazine in 1896, was even more effusive:

> The dear little place, the snug, smiling, dainty, delightful little watering-place, deserves a 'boom' and shall have it. It is, in truth, a witching, affectionate sympathetic spot . . . Until five years ago, the Pwllhelians were quite content with their quiet grey old town of narrow winding streets, over-hung by ancient houses and beetling grey cliffs, and with its harbour in the shadow of the Gimlet Rock. Then these gallant Welshmen determined to make a seaside resort of their pretty home, and they have begun with an energy and a purpose that promises well for the future . . .

She goes on at great length to praise the beaches, the view, the 'unconquered savagery' of the mountains across the bay, and even what she seems to have regarded as the unique colours of the sea at Pwllheli.

The dream, however, was never realised. The concept of a flourishing, commercialised seafront, on the model of Llandudno, one of the most powerful of Victorian seaside magnets, never got beyond the few houses at the South Beach end of the concrete promenade and the equally disconnected houses around the West End Hotel at the other end; in between, from end to end, the gorse and tufted sand remained undisturbed.

Solomon Andrews, an entrepreneur from Cardiff, built his imposing houses, named the route that leads back into the town 'Cardiff Road', created the Recreation Ground, the golf course, public tennis courts, and finally instigated the creation of the resort's crowning glory at the turn of the century, a tramway along the seafront all the way to Llanbedrog, along which my grandmother certainly travelled, wrapped up against the bitter wind, to the jingle of harness and the excitement of alien English voices.

And that's where it seems to have stopped. The glittering prospects opened up by the enthusiasm of the *Gentlewoman* and the Great Western Railway guide petered out, and Pwllheli was left once again to be Llŷn's town. Until Billy Butlin arrived. Whether or not he knew of earlier dreams when he was looking for likely sites for his working-class holiday camps in the 1940s, Mr Butlin eventually brought to fruition the commercial dreams of Solomon Andrews. Even then, the perverse fate that seems to have dogged all the town's efforts to exalt itself intervened. Butlin's camp was established some three miles outside the town on a site vacated by the Royal Navy at the end of the war, and although it brought some trade into the locality, it was, by and large, self-sufficient, and left South Beach and the West End as sleepy as ever.

Although tinged to some extent by early visions of the first Butlinites riding through the streets on brightly-coloured tandem bicycles wearing funny hats, my own memories of the town have little connection with its uncertain history. They are rather the memories of one for whom Pwllheli was 'Y Dref', and they are memories unspoilt by any hint of inadequacy.

Market day in Pwllheli is Wednesday, and on Wednesday afternoons local buses moved to town along the network of lanes and by-roads that criss-cross the peninsula. During the school holidays, along with everybody else, I would travel on the one o'clock bus operated not by impersonal Crosville, but by the Caelloi bus company, who now run flourishing continental tours in modern luxury coaches. In those days, Caelloi was a local bus company, plying between Dinas, at the foot of Garn Fadryn, and Pwllheli, employing individualists as drivers, and given to eccentricity in the nature of the buses themselves. I certainly remember travelling to Pwllheli on the wing on one occasion, when business was particularly brisk; raindrops dribbled through the roof from time to time, and the provident carried umbrellas on a rainy day. There were also occasions when a bus had to be partially emptied before it could complete the ascent of one or other of the sharp climbs it had to negotiate. But Caelloi was a company that provided a service. As its buses manoeuvred around the many corners between untrimmed hedges heavy with gorse and bramble and lush with wild flowers in spring and summer, it would stop and hoot when a regular customer failed to appear at her gate with her shopping basket. I remember more than one occasion when the driver would jump out and knock at some farm door in order to discover whether Jane Jones was coming to town that day. Similarly, although it was some years before I was allowed to experience that for myself, the last bus would never leave town at night before every effort was made to ensure that all those who had ventured out that day would also be taken back to the safety of the countryside.

We travelled to town on Wednesdays, as I said, on the one o'clock bus. And, having arrived in Y Maes among all the other buses arriving from Nefyn and Aberdaron and Abersoch and Llangwnadl, the first thing to do was to explore the stalls on Y Maes itself, and the funfair at the far end, next to the slaughterhouse. (I still suppress a slight shudder as I pass that slaughterhouse, for it was one of my hell-images as a child – forced by some sadistic gang-boss to peep through a crack in the door at the moment when the knife went in. I was long haunted by what I saw, and have never forgotten it.) As post-war austerity faded away, Y Maes was increasingly crowded with a wide variety of stalls on a Wednesday afternoon, including the mobile auction-rooms of salesmen from Manchester who off-loaded surplus goods at a break-neck pace by conducting mock auctions from the steps of their vans, eventually selling their tea-services and cutlery-sets at bargain prices.

> Here y'are, luv, you'll never see another like it. Not at this price, y'won't. I'm not asking five pounds for it; not three pounds. Tell y'what, I'll offer it – gawd, I'm cheating myself, I'll offer it for one pound ten.

A brief pause for reactions – brief enough to ensure that there couldn't be any!

> Wot! Well, I never knew such a crowd. All right then, all right then. Give me one pound note, one pound note and they're yours. Come on 'en.

Someone, of course, jumps, and they're off. Having given the impression that this is one bargain-price cutlery-set, he then brings out the others from behind him, one after the other, as the pound notes wave like leaves in the wind and his assistants scamper around, hard-faced, dispassionate observers of the gullible scene.

This happened during my adolescence, and was, I suppose, a symptom of a changing world. When I was younger, the market would be smaller, and the voices would be Welsh, although probably speaking in the foreign tones of Caernarfon, urban and easily recognisable, selling fabrics and rock. After sauntering around Y Maes, we would wander into town, where the voices were all Welsh, and where groups stood and chatted, oblivious, blocking the pavements, doing insurance business outside Woolworths and courting cagily in Caroline Cafe. Around teatime, we would go in search of chips, and then contentedly to the pictures, until, once again, adolescence brought changes, and ostensible trips to the pictures turned out to be shy, often tongue-tied and disastrous walks with pairs of girls in the general direction of South Beach. Then back home to the dark countryside, where there were no street-lamps, nothing but the stars to direct one's steps a mile or more from bus-stop home. Nowadays I still experience a sharp reminder of those days when I see a farm labourer of sixty, in tweeds and narrow tie, walking aimlessly but not unhappily from counter to counter, buttons to lingerie to pop records, and I know that he is performing the same ritual. He is going round Woolworths, and Wednesday is still an occasion, and Llŷn is still his world.

On Saturday, the visit to Pwllheli was different. It was a visit to the football match. In the villages, we played football midweek (I only played cricket at school and college). The only game we played in Llŷn was soccer. On Saturdays we came to support Pwllheli. And, of course, later, to walk the town once more, in varying ways, depending on our age. In my boyhood, Pwllheli and District was emerging from historic feebleness into unaccustomed fame, and so the youth of Llŷn began to flock to the Recreation Ground, and even hardened veterans like my father, who had once played for a real team, Caernarfon Town, and who had previously taken me to see Bangor City, and Everton in September, began to take a reluctant and disbelieving interest. The change was caused by a new phenomenon, the player-manager. In pre-television days, local clubs could contemplate a minor boom in those areas where the concept of leisure was also a new and novel thing, and the first player-manager that I recall in Pwllheli was an ex-Charlton wing-half, who, it was rumoured, had once played for Wales. He was burly and determined, but lacked speed. The team he gathered around him was similar, a few veteran ex-professionals surrounded by veteran amateurs. But it did generate interest. My father and I, however, did not join the band-wagon until the revolution happened. And the revolution was called Tommy Jones.

I am still at a loss to understand, no doubt others who were nearer the centre of affairs at the time could explain very easily, why a player of the calibre of Tommy Jones, at the age of twenty-nine, should have chosen to come to Pwllheli. I am, in any case, not concerned with such historical puzzles. Enough that he came, that he was, at that time, one of the great footballers of his era, at the peak of his form, having been the centre of a great half-back line at Everton, and having been known as a player of style and finesse. His coming was exciting, and he brought with him players of competence from Merseyside and, as time went on, attracted Welsh amateurs of talent. For some years, the fortunes of Pwllheli and District soared; they won the Welsh League North year after year and challenged the supremacy of Rhyl as the then premier team of North Wales. They often attracted crowds that many league sides would now be happy enough to see, and so they formed an integral part of our Saturdays.

The Recreation Ground is a windswept, cold field, with the sound of the sea scraping pebbles on the open shore a background theme throughout the game. I can remember the individual members of that team more clearly than perhaps any other group of people. There was, in particular, a hard, uncultured, old-fashioned full-back from Llŷn itself, who went under the name 'Tarw Nefyn' and who was a throwback to the old, bad days of Pwllheli football; and there was an inside left of great trickery who had played in the lower regions of the League and would no doubt have gone even further had it not been for an inability to distribute the ball to any constructive purpose once he had completed his circus tricks; there was also a centre-forward of character, a heavy man when seen off the football field, a man who walked stiff-legged and awkward in his civilian clothes. On the field, he was slow and deliberate enough, but his job was simply to score. He would lurk around the edge of the penalty area, and anything that came to his right foot when he had a yard or so to move was a goal. He would have been useless in a higher class of football – he would not have been given the space he needed – but in that class he was lethal. He was also a sportsman of Corinthian nobility. One particular Saturday, he had been dropped from the team, as sometimes happened as the result of a love-hate relationship that existed between him and the manager. The mistake was always made good the following week, after a less convincing team display than usual, and after it had been once again seen how empty was the opponents' penalty area in his absence. But there were Saturdays when such absences happened. On this occasion, he was watching the match behind one of the goals, and some time during the first half, a section of the crowd behind him, spotting him, began to chant, happily and loudly, 'We want . . .'; he turned and grinned. A little later, however, they changed their tune, and began to chant derisory remarks about his replacement. He went up to them rapidly and angrily, and berated them at length and to such good effect that nothing more was heard from them.

And then there was Tommy Jones himself. Nothing got past him in the air; he was not only the complete stopper of any crossed ball, and of any hopefully-lofted through ball; he would rise in such a controlled manner to high balls that he would have time to nod his clearance to the feet of the wing halves he had taught to accept such offerings, and I have seen goals of classic simplicity scored out of their own penalty area by that Pwllheli team as a headed clearance was flicked to an advancing wing half, pushed inside the fullback for the orthodox left-winger (ex-Everton also) to pull it back for the centre forward to kill it stone dead with his left foot and plant it with calm inevitability in the corner of the net with his right.

I left the Recreation Ground on those afternoons as reluctantly as I leave it now. But the game did eventually end, and we did move back into the town. In the days before football fever gripped me, I would spend Saturday afternoon at the cinema, in the children's matinee. And all that has ever been written of children's matinees, of the cheers and counter-cheers as heroes came and went on the screen, was true of the Palladium at Pwllheli.

Early space fantasies followed the cowboy film, especially 'Flash Gordon'. Every Saturday afternoon, Flash was left tied to some devilish laboratory contraption, about to be exterminated by a variety of death-rays. Madly excited by all this inside the cinema, we left to catch the four-fifteen home for tea, and to play versions of 'Flash Gordon' in the garden until bedtime. It was a crucial step towards manhood when we stopped going to the Saturday matinee, went to the football instead, and later visited the first-house pictures and travelled home on the eight o'clock bus. Travelling into town from Llaniestyn with a friend, watching the older girls climb on in pairs at remote bus stops, the excitement of the trip always gripped us. We stared entranced at these gorgeous dark-haired creatures, tall and precarious in their shiny high heels, old and awesome in their silk stockings, pale and remote in powder and paint. And we watched as they minced their way off the bus in Pwllheli and joined the circulating courting ritual around the streets. Boys would be met, if at all, at dusk in chip-shops, or inside the cinema when a firm arrangement had been made. It was all conducted surreptitiously, mysteriously, a cause of amused, supposedly disapproving speculation to the adults who left for home, loaded with bags and baskets, on the four o'clock bus. As soon as we too began to go to the first-house, neighbours, aunts and grandmothers began to say, 'Who's the lucky girl then?' 'Oh, he's got someone in that Pwllheli, don't worry.' 'We'll soon find out, don't you fret.' And we mused sadly on how this was to be achieved, how we could justify their happy suspicions. Meanwhile we watched and waited and consoled ourselves with the heroic sunsets of Hollywood. The last stage in this whole process, of course, and the result of protracted negotiation, was to borrow my father's car and get home no later than I would have arrived had I taken the last bus; but this was in the dim future, after many walks home in the dark rain from the bus stop by Rhydbach Chapel.

The atmosphere in the first-house was certainly very different from the raucous racket in the matinee, whichever picture-house one went to; but there was also a considerable difference between the two cinemas. Normally, one went to the Palladium, but there was also the Town Cinema, a part-time function of the Town Hall, where plays, concerts, and various kinds of other entertainments took place. The Town Cinema was rough and ready, and had the reputation of sometimes showing what were then thought to be daring films. It also had the added facility, for courting couples, of having galleries running down each side, unlit by the flickering images from the screen, undisturbed by wanderers in and out, consistently and comfortably dark. It was a mildly adventurous undertaking to visit the Town Hall.

Pwllheli was the chip-shop, was two cinemas and a football ground, and this was what a town was. One point about it, of course, which escaped our notice then, but which is clear enough now, was that all the shops were independent, run by their owners, and almost all were centres of social discourse. I can picture in practically all the shops in town the unchanging face and manner of the server behind the counter. It was an unchanging town; the shop-fronts did not change, ownership did not vary and there was a sense of permanence about the sights and sounds of every street.

Walking up Gaol Street towards the hill dominated by the old grammar school building, I knew that I would find the particular comic I wanted in Caxton House on the corner; I wouldn't have visited that shop otherwise, because the owner, bespectacled and not easily given to smiling, making clear his dislike of small boys, made any simple purchase a considerable ordeal. Higher up was Miss Clarke's fish shop, where fried mushrooms were also sold, and where the old lady was helped by sturdy married sons – and probably daughters-in-law – who really did run fishing boats, and at least one of whom played for Pwllheli and District in its amateur days. *Siop* Miss Clarke, with its haddock and its readiness to buy, as well as sell, mushrooms which we gathered in Llŷn, was a mark of permanence. A few doors further up was the empty, grim window of the bone-setter, another permanent feature of the landscape. He still travelled around practising his craft, but his era was even then coming to an end. We walked past the skull in his window and continued up the comfortable, unchanging street.

At the far end, beyond the Whitehall Hotel, round the corner into High Street, we came upon the hand-sized cloud in that clear sky of certainty, Woolworths, the trailblazer for Spar and Lo Cost and all their kind. And yet Woolworths didn't seem to us to be an interloper. It was where everyone met. On the pavement outside, people waited for their friends. It was in Woolworths that the best range of sweets and chocolates was on display, it was in Woolworths that one was most likely to meet by fortunate chance whoever one was most eager to meet. Subtly and quietly, it had already taken over; it was the cloud on a blue horizon. Life was already changing, although we didn't know it; an era was already coming to an end.

As for the two of us, disgorging with all the other country lads onto Y Maes in the dusk of a winter afternoon, we walked the streets like everyone else, went for chips, and eventually found the confidence to tackle the town girls, snooty and confident, only half-Welsh, sizing up our potential for exploitation.

'Where you from then?'

'Llaniestyn.'

'Where?'

'Look, he can talk.'

'Can't do anything else though, can 'e?'

And they would stroll off, laughing, chewing gum, swinging their bottoms dismissively at us. To begin with we would watch them go, dismayed and blushing. But then, like many another before us, we learnt how to shout back, and swagger away in our turn.

After I had gone off to boarding-school, I was able to generate a certain amount of curious envy

– a thing unheard of among my acquaintances in Llŷn.

'Where d'you go to school then?'

'Shwsbri.'

'What for?'

'I dunno.'

'E's a bad boy. That's what them schools are for. E's been caught stealing and sent away.'

'I have not.'

'Yes, you have.'

'Why've you been sent away?'

'I haven't then.'

A thin girl with pigtails, an Irish girl who had come to Llŷn, also interested herself in me, listening and biting her nails when the topic of boarding-schools cropped up. She wasn't Llŷn-born. She was the eldest of a family of nine pale Irish children who had moved into a damp cottage near the church in Llaniestyn. She was one of the inexplicable and unquestioned phenomena of war. Her father had been invalided out of the Army, pale as his children, racked by a permanent cough. She, Patricia let us call her, would look at me through long lashes.

'They whip them on the bum in them schools.'

'Don't be silly . . .'

'They do. Seen it on the flicks. Take their pants down . . .'

'No . . .'

''Ave they done it to you then?'

They did and they had, but I wasn't prepared to admit it to her or to anyone else. Not at that stage in our relationship anyhow. I would laugh uneasily and turn away. The curiosity I had generated was not then to my liking. Some years later, a crowd of us, adolescents and children alike, took it into our heads to climb Garn Fadryn on a fine summer-holiday afternoon, taking a rudimentary picnic with us, and dragging the little ones by main force through bracken twice as high as their heads. We eventually reached the wide green shoulder below the summit where everyone rushed around, searching for a well-known spring of clear water, climbing the huge flat slab called Arthur's Table, playing tick and stumbling into hidden foxholes. Patricia and I sat apart from the rest that afternoon, looking out over the green meadows to the sea at Porthdinllaen. I watched her long fingers twining in the grass and her slim, grubby legs bent beneath her.

'Where will you be,' she asked, 'twenty years from now?'

'God, I don't know,' I said, with a boy's contempt for fantasy. These were girls' concerns.

'I'm going back to Ireland.'

'To Ireland?' I was amazed. My interest was aroused.

'It's only over there. You can see the Wicklow Hills when it's clear. Maybe I can see them now. See? Just below that cloud. It is! It's the Wicklow Hills.'

'What do you want to go to Ireland for?'

'What for? Doesn't my mother live there?'

Her strange way of talking had always fascinated me, but the content was now stranger than the style.

'Your mother? But she lives in Llaniestyn."

'That's not my mother, silly. That's only my father's woman. We call her Mary. They can't marry because my father's a Catholic. But they love each other all right.'

These were deep waters, too deep for me, in my sheltered complacency, to cope with. Then she turned her green eyes on me. 'You won't be here either, will you? You'll be a big important man somewhere twenty years from now.'

'Don't be soft.'

'Give me a kiss, in case we never see each other again.'

And she closed her eyes and held her pursed red lips out to me. And so I kissed her, the first time I had kissed a girl, and I tasted the softness of another's sweet nervousness and seemed for a moment to have an inkling of our common mortality.

'Will you hold my hand on the way down?' she asked. How could I refuse? Although the sniggers of the young ones as they watched our blushes caused me more pain than she knew. Her whole family moved very soon after that, and I never saw her again. I think of her sometimes still, looking out over the Irish sea on a clear summer evening, when the vague outline of the Wicklow Hills can just be seen.

# II

I have many homes in Llŷn. My father spent much of his adult life as an Anglican parson in various parts of the peninsula. This placed me in an ambivalent position. The Anglican Communion, for all its inheritance of ancient grey churches that seem to grow out of the earth, cannot be greatly commended for its part in Welsh history. Wales never took kindly to the Reformation of Thomas Cromwell. In many ways the Methodist Revival of the eighteenth century stepped neatly over the intervening centuries to grasp the true social meaning of Celtic Christianity, its commitment to the transformation of community life in Wales. Such a commitment was certainly as necessary in the eighteenth century as it had been in the fifth, when the pioneering army of militant Christians walked in from the sea and built churches whose descendants still stand in the same circular graveyards.

In the course of time, the Church of England inherited these churches and their history, usually without realising the nature of its heritage, certainly without nurturing the indigenous culture that had been so closely associated in the past with Christian belief. Solitary and unhonoured clergy strove to maintain the link, but they did not represent the established philosophy of their church in these matters, much given to the aping of English manners and customs and to the insistent use of the English language, even in predominantly Welsh-speaking areas. Nevertheless, the link was tenuously retained, and the number of Welsh Anglicans who knew and respected the nature of their heritage grew. In Llŷn, set apart as it was, there had always been a strong sense of the past in the Anglican Church's adherence to the Welsh language, even though the scholarly squire-parson who jingled along between the high hedges in his coach and pair was far removed from the ascetic missionaries from whom he was descended.

My father was brought up in a Methodist household in a slate-quarrying village, paradoxically named Cwm-y-Glo, in Eryri. He became a passionate Anglican as the result of a stormy reaction against what he regarded as the hypocrisy and moral corruption of Methodist mores. In common with all such decisions, his was triggered off by more than one personal complex. His mother had undoubtedly been harshly treated by the chapel community for she was unmarried, and he was born out of wedlock. I do not know to this day who his father was. The foster-parents who brought him up seem themselves to have been rebels against the dishonesty of what was peculiarly termed 'temperance' and the requirement that was still in force for chapel members to sign the teetotal pledge. My father's own form of rebelliousness was to climb out of bedroom windows to play football, contrary to orders, and ultimately to reject the chapel altogether. He fell an easy prey to the recruiting bands and Kitchener posters, went early to war and came home a quartermaster sergeant at nineteen, with more than a touch of military grandiosity about him, a trait he never lost. He went to work on the railway, but always with the ambition of going to college. When he eventually achieved his ambition, it was all-of-a-piece with his by now ambivalent attitude to his upbringing that a succession of setbacks led him, not to the University College in Bangor, but to a theological college in England. His rejection of Methodism was becoming to some extent a rejection of Welshness altogether. He was acquiring, entirely Welsh as he was, some of the characteristics of an adopted Anglican Tory. He never lost these characteristics either, even when in his later years he decided that the time had come to vote, with many misgivings, for Plaid Cymru. As a Tory, he was a high Tory. He regarded society as a well-ordered map, and believed in the ruling classes. And as a churchman he was a high churchman, what he himself insisted on terming a 'catholic'. Even as a football fan, these traits of high emotionalism and absolute belief in the ultimate rightness of things shone through – his football fields were peopled by giants, ogres and fairy-kings even when he was a grown man. Issues were still clear and uncomplicated; people were still good and bad.

I, in turn, was brought up with this colourful concept of life as my working model. Brought up as well, however, with memories, not of a black-garbed, god-fearing parsonical figure, but of a sweatered cursing presence, constantly involved in make-do-and-mend. We were fated to live, not in regular vicarages, but in a succession of makeshift substitutes, ranging from a small, red-roofed bungalow in Bryncroes to a splendid, but crumbling, Tudor dower-house near Botwnog. In all these places, my father was the man who had to reduce external shambles – brambles, overgrown plants, weed-covered drives, fallen treetrunks – to a manageable level, and my mother had to brighten up internal decay with constant patching. It was a period when ancient vehicles were the order of the day on the roads of Llŷn, and my father's cars were never good in the morning, and never really built to travel further than Pwllheli. He would forge close friendships with mechanics, in Rhoshirwaun, in Sarn, in Morfa Nefyn, and he would spend whole mornings standing in freezing garages philosophizing at length with them all. And days and days were spent hoeing and raking long gravel drives. He spent so much time at these activities that prying tourists, coming upon the old house and marvelling, took him for the handyman and paid him half-a-crown for his trouble. He always pocketed such unsolicited gifts and touched his forelock dutifully. I can see him in his tattered grey sweater, the one sweater that lived on through my childhood and adolescence, a thick-set, dark, stocky, powerful man, totally engrossed in purely physical activity, mending lawn-mowers, sweeping up the eternal tide of fallen leaves, meticulously measuring the right proportion of weedkiller to pour into an ancient watering can without possessing the right measuring instruments, fighting a long battle against the odds of an uncooperative environment. Had he been a scholar by nature, or one of the English gentlemen he so admired, he must have been deeply wounded by such an existence. Fortunately, he was made of sterner stuff.

My mother and I, when I was very small, would commute a good deal to what was a sort of family base in Morfa Nefyn. We would start from Bryncroes in an ancient Austin 7, so desperately cold in winter that I would have to wear gloves and then bury my gloved hands deep in my coat pockets. I could only just see above the dashboard, and I mapped my mother's erratic progress along the lanes of Llŷn by the changing skylines of the hedgerows, from high, bare earthen walls to waving banks of gorse to the black scaffolding of whitethorn in its bare winter harshness. And patterns of bird passage would cross my vision also as I sat there, hunched and bouncing rhythmically to the little car's movement – crows hovering and seagulls, on stormy days, drifting inland for shelter. When I grew a little older, I came to know Nefyn a good deal better, for my father abruptly removed me from the primary school at Dinas and deposited me at my grandmother's from Monday to Friday so that I could attend the school at Morfa Nefyn. More of that in its own good time, for it eventually led to my removal from Llŷn's Council Schools altogether, and to the ultimate trauma of a boarding school in Shrewsbury. My grandparents on my mother's side had originally lived in Eifionydd. My grandfather was a blacksmith in Pant Glas. Pant Glas is a forsaken strip of a village on the peatland route that stretches from Caernarfon to Porthmadog, across damp, stony, unproductive earth where scattered smallholdings struggled then to produce minimal crops and where life was basic. Whole clutches of children in these localities, brothers and sisters, died of tuberculosis within months of each other, defeated by weakness, desperately under-nourished. I have seen their names on gravestones and I have seen their faces staring out from yellowed photographs, sapped of energy, dulled, yet sometimes still showing the impishness of childhood behind tired eyes. My mother's family did not escape. I never knew my grandfather, but he stands in these ancient photographs four-square to the camera, moustachioed, even crudely elegant, obviously enjoying it, and I am not surprised that he and my father were firm friends. But he wasn't physically equipped for the demands of a smithy, and in the end it killed him. He married the daughter of a formidable lady who ran a public house single-handed some miles up the road in Glandwyfach, and who was known for the awesome authority she displayed in disposing of incipient drunkards. She served glasses of water to those she deemed to have reached their limit, and no one was ever supposed to have failed to take the hint. This is not to say that ugly scenes did not take place in Glandwyfach, and in fact my grandmother, who used to help in the bar and do the chores, as befitted a healthy girl, was conditioned into a deep hatred of alcohol by her experience there, and never again entered a pub during the course of a long life.

My grandparents had four children, three boys and a girl, my mother being the eldest. Griff, the eldest boy, was apprenticed to his father, Emrys, the next one, went to work on the farm, and John, the youngest, became a gardener. None of them was regarded as likely to prosper in school, and I doubt if they were encouraged to do so. Griff was beset by asthma from early days, and when it was clear that he would not be able to take over the smithy, he too was sent off to the open-air life of gardening. Being a gardener for the gentry was, after all, lighter work than out-and-out farming, and as secure as anything could be in those captive years. When my grandfather died in middle age, worn through by the heat and the hammer, my grandmother took the family, lock stock and barrel, to Llŷn, established herself in a sizeable house in Morfa Nefyn, and set about keeping 'visitors'.

Our visits to Nefyn naturally centred on the tea-table, for the tradition of obligatory hospitality and constant eating of scones and home-baked bread and currant tarts was still strong. My grandmother never ate with us; she had retained the rural traditions of Eifionydd even in the semi-urban sophistication of Nefyn. It was not done for the lady of the house to eat with guests, not even when the guests were family. Her function was to ply everyone else with food and then snatch what spare mouthfuls she could later in the privacy of the kitchen. I have seen the same pattern repeated again and again in the farms of Llŷn; it may still happen for all I know. Griff, though, often seems in my memory to be at table with us, and it was there, sitting on the huge settle, swinging my feet above the tiled floor, that he first figured in my life. He would draw pictures with golden syrup on my bread and butter – the picture of a lion, the picture of a house – and he would constantly ply me with puzzles devised with combinations of matches. Pouring the matches onto the table, off he would go – 'Right, there's eleven horses and you've got to get them into ten stables. This match is the first horse . . .' Or he would sit, after tea, on the wooden stool by the fire and make spills with strips of newspaper, twisting the paper skilfully around his fingers until he had a boxful of match-saving fire-lighters. Matches no doubt had to be reserved for puzzles and tricks. Then he would ceremonially hand me a spill so that I could dip it into the flames and hold it to his pipe while he puffed and huffed and filled the little room with the marvellous pungency of tobacco-smoke. One day he took me to see Lloyd George. I must have been about five or six, and Lloyd George, still a great mythic figure in Llŷn, was attending the Nefyn Show. I remember his car rolling in, and the uniformed chauffeur coming out and opening the car boot and turning it into a speaker's rostrum. The old man, white hair streaming in the wind, mounted the platform, stick in hand, and began to speak. I sat on Griff's shoulders so that I could see him properly. Lloyd George, said Griff, would be coming to my grandmother's for tea.

'Where's Lloyd George?' I asked later, safe on the settle, my feet dangling.

'Lloyd George? What's the matter with the boy?' My grandmother was not unduly concerned. She was accustomed to my eccentric questioning.

'Can I go and see if he's coming?'

'You sit there and eat your tea.'

'But Nain, when is he coming?'

'Don't be silly now.'

'But Uncle Griff said . . .'

'What have you been telling the boy?'

But Griff simply sat on the stool by the fire, stoking up his pipe and smiling contentedly. The fact that Lloyd George never came did not shake my confidence in Griff. It was Lloyd George who had let me down, that old man with the white hair and the raised walking-stick who had shouted at us all from the boot of his car. My mother was already married when the others arrived in Nefyn. She had moved up in the world, as Dick Jones had now, finally, become a parson. Griff found a job in a hotel, Emrys was sent off to work on a farm near Caernarfon, and John learned a new trade and became the local barber. My grandmother, something of a tyrant, kept a close eye on them all, including my mother, and so it was that we commuted there regularly, eldest daughter and first, prized, protected grandson, bearing gifts to the throne. My father came less frequently, not only because the demands of his calling kept him at home, but because the ambivalence that dogged him all his life was here too in evidence. The almost aggressive catch-as-catch-can lifestyle of the household, scratching a livelihood here and there, dominated by the need to consolidate their escape from poverty, and watched and harried in the process by their mother, offended his romantic concept that life ought to be different, contradicted his determined belief in a divine order. And so he stayed in his wild gardens and weed-ridden drives, hacking away at the growth and treasuring his independence, his own escape from his own past into however ironic and dilapidated a dignity.

It was true that he had created for himself an independent life. For all its ambivalence, there could be no more unstructured an existence than the life of a country parson in the hinterland of Llŷn. A lesser man than my father might, it is true, have been defeated by the prospect of maintaining even the shreds of a dignified independence without that automatic inherited affluence which enabled his predecessors in massive vicarages to create comfortable insulation for themselves and establish often unearned reputations as mysterious but formidable scholars. He was not, in the final analysis, defeated. He remained his own man, fed by his dislike of the sloppiness of the Welsh life he knew, its inefficiency and its petty hypocrisy, and fortified by his dreams of a wider world, a wider world which I, for one, was to occupy. He had an inordinately high regard for the English, but he himself was irredeemably

Welsh. Welsh was his native language, and he certainly made no attempt to turn his back on that fact. Self-educated, an avid and indiscriminate bookworm, he was well-versed in the history of the Celtic Church, and indeed in the whole history of Wales, biased and colourful though his version of it was. He knew a great deal about ecclesiastical architecture and he was an energetically prejudiced observer of the world scene.

Sometimes he seemed impregnable. But there were times when the mask would slip, and I can remember some of them well. I remember returning from a Nefyn visit to our bungalow in Bryncroes. We lived then in the open reaches of Llŷn, beyond Garn Fadryn, in a no-man's land of small fields and ditches, criss-crossed with gorse and blackthorn hedges. Anyone who might suppose in midwinter that this was a bleak, God-forsaken place, and who might even say in August that it was burnt and brown and shrivelled, should see the driven whiteness of blackthorn in spring in places where fields are small and hedges seem to sit one on top of another all the way back to the purple rocks of Mynydd Rhiw. And the only relieving feature of this unnatural flood of white is the equal violence of the gorse, thrusting yellow all around. Drive from Rhoshirwaun to Nefyn in spring and it batters at your eyes, an unsophisticated burst of creative life rising out of poor soil, where rocks lurk close to the surface and where the rain sweeps from the sea through the mist in winter. We had been to Nefyn in the Austin 7 (or the Morris 8 – elderly cars followed so close on the heels of one another, it is difficult to place any of them very precisely) and I think we must have stayed there for some days. My father had bought an ancient motorbike, so that, for the first and last time, we were a two-vehicle family, and I remember returning at night to find him sitting grey and weary by the kitchen fire, a walking stick in his hand, looking at us with something like desperation in his eyes.

He had crashed on his bike some days before, and been driven home by a passer-by, leaving the wreck in the hedge. His hip had stiffened and he had spent three days dragging himself to and from the all-night stove, and making himself cups of tea. In the middle of all this his dog, Jack, who had survived city traffic and city dangers with no difficulty during our brief time on Merseyside, dragged his dying body home after picking up rat poison in someone's field and died on the doorstep. I think it was on such occasions, when fate seemed suddenly to stop smiling, that his romantic visions collapsed, and life lost all semblance of value.

The other occasion was longer-lasting, and happened much later. I was grown-up by then, and had returned home on a flying visit from somewhere, as I used to before my marriage. He had by then moved to Anglesey, and if I arrived late, which often happened, my mother would probably have gone to bed, and he would be making himself a midnight cup with slabs of thick bread and butter, which he would then take to eat before the dying embers of an open fire, and sit and drink and poke and think until the early hours. He would look forward to my fleeting visits more than he admitted, for increasingly, as I grew older, communication between us increased, and if he heard my car pull up outside, out would come a second cup, and out would come all the old prejudices. He seemed to see it as his duty to put my untried liberalism to the sternest of tests, and would plunge into matters of eternal moment. He indulged in no chit-chat, asked no questions about the whys and wheres of my life, for such details never interested him. He didn't want to know what I did; he wanted to know what I thought, and at times seemed to want to demolish it all. Around one o'clock, the fire would be cold, and we would set to with bits of paper to restoke it for another session, we would listen to the sounds of a country night, and he would go to the back door and comment systematically on the state of the night sky, and its prognostications for morning weather. The talk was never personal; he was an entirely shy man in relation to all intimacies. But in the process of unleashing our passionately held differences at each other all night long, we found a bond we had not possessed before, and occasionally even penetrated into personal comment.

On this particular occasion, things were different. I walked into the house and found him slumped before a dead fire, an old man motionless. When he saw me, he moved slowly, shuffled into his slippers, managed a sort of smile and asked whether I wanted tea. When he had made it, we sat before the cold grate, and for a long time there was silence. And then he told me, simply, and with none of his usual arrogant challenge, how a young man in the parish had committed suicide that day in a particularly violent manner, a young man he knew well, although not a churchgoer. He was broken by the realisation that he had been of no use. What, he asked, was the purpose of a priest if he couldn't be a vessel to accept the torment and desperation of people in his charge. He had failed. Over the years, he could cope with the fact that his congregations were small and dwindling, that his was in many ways a lonely and friendless existence, that he was never going to be offered any more demanding tasks than those he had grown totally accustomed to, that the great world outside would always remain a dream. But the thought that he was useless in his very function as a priest struck at the root of his being. He spoke that night, as he had never done before, of his incapacity for the only life he had ever seriously considered, that of the priesthood. He was known as a pastor; it was assumed that although he would never go to inter-denominational services, never take part in unity exercises, although he was certainly an opponent of much that he thought Welsh nonconformity stood for, indeed perhaps because of all this, his mental parish literally comprised all the souls within its geographical boundaries. He drew no distinctions between the God-fearing and the backsliding, between his own members and the members of other persuasions when it came to sick-visiting and the regular round of tea and biscuits. To have failed in this when it mattered was to have failed in everything. He never recovered his ebullience after this event, an event which no one else ever associated with him at all.

During the large portion of his time in Llŷn, my father had the care of two very old churches, Llandudwen and Llaniestyn, and was largely responsible for the restoration of another, Llangwnadl, and as I would go, in the normal course of things, to these churches to worship, or at least to sit and behave myself, it became a natural thing to be surrounded by ancient walls, and to walk in places hallowed by many centuries of religious life. It was a part, if an entirely unconscious part, of childhood in Llŷn. The services in Llaniestyn were entirely in Welsh, but those in Llandudwen were, even then, mainly in English, and I went to both. My memories of them are in no way linguistic. If I didn't know it as an historical fact, I wouldn't today remember the Englishness of Llandudwen or the Welshness of Llaniestyn. I do remember that in Llaniestyn we had a rudimentary choir and a rudimentary Band of Hope meeting on weeknights. And I remember unruly Sunday School classes where I believe I was the type of nasty, imaginative troublemaker who stuck pins in the row in front. I was certainly not a good pupil. But chiefly I remember winter nights in the old church, winter nights in wartime, when, in order to conserve fuel, my father would measure an exact amount of coupon-petrol into the small private generator that lit the church – that part of Llŷn was not yet in possession of a public electricity supply – and it was often touch and go whether the supply would last the whole service, especially if the sermon outran itself. Sometimes it didn't last, and we would go home in darkness, hastily blessed as we went, sometimes from the top of the cellar steps as my father made his way down to investigate the hiccupping generator.

Life as the parson's son in such a place and at such a time was not therefore the structured, middle-class existence of literary vicarages and sons of clergy. It was both separate and entirely involved. Separate in the physical reality of large houses; involved because of the ancient organic unity of society in Llŷn in those days. To describe it as classless would be to use the term anachronistically. There were ranks and degrees, people had their functions and they walked the paths ordained by providence. There was a stability and predictability about people's social movements that had by-passed the Industrial Revolution; the pattern of events, both for the community and the individual, was entirely dictated by the natural cycle. Apart from the largely undeveloped tourist trade, the whole locality was geared to agriculture. Those who were not farmers serviced the farming community, either as shopkeepers or teachers or ministers of religion. Social events were subservient to the needs of ploughing, sowing and harvesting; little or nothing was organized during the summer months; concerts, dramatic performances, whist drives, eisteddfodau, all took place during the long dark winter evenings, all the darker during my childhood for the imposition of the blackout. I hovered around such events, watching the adults and carrying kettles and flower vases. As I grew older, all such social gatherings during the hours of darkness provided exciting, stolen moments with elusive and beautiful girls, tossing their dark hair in the wind that always howled around village halls in Llŷn on winter nights. That constant south-westerly often carried driving rain as well, but we happily huddled in the lee of corrugated-iron porticos and under the slanting lights from the hall windows. Inside would be warm and organized, choirs singing, adults in overcoats playing cards, but outside in the cold dark we would tease out each other's responses, touch, slap and tickle in a breathless excitement and laugh uncertainly at each other's jokes, until some wondering adult would thrust a censorious head through the door and put an end to our socializing. Everything that happened happened annually, regularly, and was part of an unchanging, totally predictable cycle of events.

Human considerations and human decisions really counted for very little. Some people were no doubt regarded as being of a superior social order, but I knew no one outside the squirearchy who was rich. Rich people, people who owned luxury goods and kept servants, people who drove a great deal in polished cars lived, if at all, in Abersoch and not in the heart of Llŷn. It was an economically deprived community. That did not really register in the mind of a boy. What registered, if unconsciously was the basic sameness of everyone's lot. If, as very occasionally happened in summer, a large, new, shiny car would pass slowly through the village of Llaniestyn while we were conducting our social interchange at the church gate after the evening service, it would be regarded by us not with envy or dislike, but simply with distant curiosity. It was an intruder from another world, a world we as children never contemplated aspiring to.

Our periodic shift from one borrowed home to another, although offering an element of colour and uncertainty in practical things, nevertheless happened within the basic permanence of the same social cycle, within the prime importance of the changing seasons. The first home I remember was the small bungalow in Bryncroes, red-roofed and standing on a side-road meandering away from the main route between Sarn and Aberdaron towards Llangwnadl and the sea. My clearest memory of this period is of life at the neighbouring farm.

Lisi Brynffynnon was a tiny, lame spinster who kept house for the local carpenter and coffin-maker, Richard Jones. Richard Jones was an imposing, Victorian figure, seemingly and reputedly well-off by our standards, forever clicking his yardstick, and forever making firm, authoritative marks with a pencil on those beautiful white planks that furnished the walls of his workshop. He had a helper, an apprentice, who was in ill health, and who disappeared early from my memories, whether to die of tuberculosis or to go to war I never managed to sort out in my mind. People did disappear from our view in those days, and some never came back. Tuberculosis was still a scourge, malnutrition was still common. And young men did go to war. One house we passed with awe because the son was a prisoner-of-war in Germany, and we knew that they sent him parcels. It was, of course, a war-deprived land peopled with women, old men and sickly youths. Maybe we boys, growing free, benefited in some ways from the absence of dominant men.

Richard Jones's workshop stood in the middle of his farmyard, and it shared a long building with the cattle, who provided his other means of livelihood. For there was a sizeable smallholding attached to the house as well, a smallholding controlled by Lisi. Half a dozen cows would moo and shuffle and champ their hay next door, while I would climb up the wooden ladder from the workshop to the warm loft. There I would lie on my face and peer through the cracks at those slow, soft animals below, chewing and swallowing, munching, chewing and swallowing, while their eyes roamed around their shed as though searching for some new feature that had changed during their brief departure in the fields.

The workshop itself was stacked with planks. I could see that cut and treated wood was beautiful, and that the quality of a piece of oak was something to feel and handle and admire. I would sit half-way up the wooden ladder, on my way to my rendezvous with the cows, and watch the carpenters at work, taking a plank, slapping it down on the hacked and worn workbench, marking it, flipping it over almost one-handed, marking it again, slapping it in a vice with professional economy of movement. And on the walls of the workshop were ranged the carpenter's tools. Handles shone, not with newness, but with the constant rub and grasp of palm and fingers, and blades glittered. The slow rubbing of chisel and plane with greased cloth, the deliberate, unhurried choice of a new implement, the systematic replacement of the old. That was the rhythm of Richard Jones's life. Lisi nevertheless told me a horrific story one day when I arrived at Brynffynnon with my can to take home our quart of milk direct from the milking.

'Look at this. Come and look at this,' she said excitedly, leading me to a black scar on the kitchen wall. Richard would take a siesta every day after his dinner of potatoes and boiled ham, followed by rice pudding. He would lie full length on the wooden settle, place a handkerchief over his face and snore loudly for twenty minutes. And this particular day, a dark and thundery summer's afternoon, with the heavy clouds rolling in from the sea, Lisi had opened the lower half of the window above Richard's head to ease the stifling sultriness of the day. Lisi kept her crockery in a wicker basket on a high shelf on the other side of the kitchen. She would climb a little step-ladder, crockery balanced precariously in her arms, to place her cups and plates in this basket. As she was doing this to the accompaniment of Richard's snores, a sudden searing sound from behind her caused her to drop a cup from her pile and almost to fall off the ladder herself. At the same time, the whole room was blindingly filled with light. While Richard snored, lightning had come in through the window, hit the opposite wall and bounced back over his head to depart once more through the window whence it came. Lisi shakingly showed me the broken cup as living proof of the story. Richard slept on, the even tenor of his life undisturbed.

But my real friend was Lisi herself. Sometime during that period in Bryncroes, pneumonia prevailing where lightning had failed, Richard Jones died. The house and farm and all his worldly possessions passed to Lisi, and the workshop stood empty and unused, just as he had left it. Whether anyone was given the tools or the wood I don't remember; all I remember was the sudden silence when he became ill. The death of the workshop preceded Richard Jones's own death only by a month or two. But the cows lived on, calves came and went in the little pen at the side of the cowshed, and I continued to jump in and fondle them in the manured hay. Consequently I caught ringworm, which was promptly and efficiently cured by a patent, home-made ointment of Lisi's own making that she kept high up on a shelf in the kitchen. The main ingredient, I believe, was seaweed, gathered by Lisi herself from the rocks at Llangwnadl.

I think someone must have come to till the fields, for things, I remember, did grow. But my interest was confined to the yard, the cowshed where Lisi carried her three-legged stool from cow to cow and set to work on their udders with her rapid fingers, and the kitchen, where I learnt to drink buttermilk, to eat salted, new-made butter, and home-made bread, to drink half a cupful of that rich milk intended by nature for the newborn calf. I would sit for hours in the warm kitchen, where the kettle simmered permanently on the hob and some kind of cawl bubbled away in a cast-iron cauldron, and the only sweets on offer were huge mint imperials. When visitors came, which was fairly often, Lisi put on her spectacles and read to them from the varied newspapers and magazines delivered to her by all and sundry. They were mainly chapel publications, the local weekly and the only English intruder, the *Liverpool Daily Post*, which I think she took about four times a week.

It was also at Bryncroes that I remember the desolation of the first time I returned home from school to find the house empty and mother gone. I used to walk to school. And school was about two miles away. A big dark girl from further along the road, a girl called Mair, came and called for me to begin with, for there was a stretch of main road to negotiate, before we dived off again onto byroads, and eventually came upon the hidden hamlet of Bryncroes itself. But soon I became independent, and went myself. And as I came down the final stretch of main road towards the red-roofed bungalow, I could see the smoke rising from the chimney, and I would begin to forget about throwing stones at telegraph poles and hunting the lizards in the hedges, and hurry home for tea. I can still feel the lurch of panic and the sick emptiness in my stomach the first time I looked at the chimney-stack and saw no smoke emerging.

The house seemed out of place. I sensed the desolation of the locality for the first time. I clenched my fists and started to run, talking breathlessly to myself. I think it was that day, as the locked door confirmed the horror, that I realised there were other sources of comfort and other kindly realities outside home. I dashed, weeping desperately, to Lisi, and she made tea, and my mother came and the world righted itself, and it was all an episode, no more. But I can glance now at a smokeless chimney-pot and feel that spasm of terror which is the first intimation that there is no one in the end that can stand between you and the loneliness of growing up.

# III

My second home was at the foot of Garn Fadryn, in the still trough of the peninsula. We moved there, I believe, when I was seven. My father had become the Rector of Llaniestyn, but the rectory, a long, dark house, was not then fit for habitation. Built for squire-parsons, with adjacent stables and rambling gardens, it had fallen into sulky disrepair. And so, by a combination of circumstances which certainly involved the fairy godmother who was to loom large in my life later, Mrs Gough, the widowed lady of the manor at Nanhoron, we came to live at the foot of Garn Fadryn.

The house was big. Built of granite by an Englishman in 1907, it was once called Ravenscourt. My father now painted a sign in English, 'The Rectory', and spent a careful morning with screws and screwdriver, firmly fixing it to the gate while I watched. All around the house were laurel bushes, and a small orchard. There was even a field where I played solitary football, close by molehills and bramble thickets. And my mother, for a time, kept geese. Geese, of course, can be violent. And for a horrific week or more my mother was forbidden access to her own field by the vituperative hissing of an angry gander. We could see Porthdinllaen quite clearly and the coastguards' houses on the hill at Morfa Nefyn, for the land fell away northwards for five miles, all the way to the sea. And I could see the Skerries light, winking through my window at regular intervals on stormy nights when the wind easily carried the sound of the sea to my bed. In bed, I could hear the heavy drone of aircraft flying overhead. They were on their way, my mother said, to bomb Liverpool. And sometimes I would creep to the window, and watch the searchlights swinging across the blackness above and beyond Eryri. It was all happening too far away to matter to me. There was just one occasion when a German bomber, no doubt fleeing from a pursuing fighter, crashed into the mountainside, and the L.D.V., still without uniform, but with important armbands, had to trudge up to the shattered remains and stand guard over them until soldiers came to look and poke at the wreckage. Then they all went away, and we children descended on the carcass. I secured a clock, and a piece of fuselage with a tiny remnant of the German insignia painted on it. I took it home enthusiastically, and was lectured for looting. The L.D.V., of course, later became the Home Guard. In our part of Llŷn, they were commanded by an Englishman who lived in a large house in Nefyn called Cliff Castle. His name was Colonel O'Farrell. We would watch them marching up and down in their patchwork uniforms and then go away and imitate them, especially the moustachioed O'Farrell, with his brisk little steps, his silver-topped stick and his incomprehensible accent. The drill instructions were given in a different kind of English by monolingual Welsh corporals: 'Leff, Reit, Leff, Reit, Holt! Ordar Amss!' Their ranks would sometimes be augmented by young men who had been returned home from the real Army on the grounds that their understanding of proper English was insufficient to ensure that they could respond to orders without causing chaos among their comrades. Their understanding was quite adequate for the Home Guard in Llŷn.

Soon I myself came firmly into contact with the English language, entrancingly mysterious and spoken by evacuees. The evacuees arrived in Sarn, three miles away, having been loaded into buses at Pwllheli station, and driven off into the unlit, frightening countryside. The confusion when they arrived in Sarn was bliss to behold when my father and I drove down to see the buses drive in. Although I was forcefully instructed to remain inside our Austin and had to peer out at the amazing scene through steamy windows, I was stunned. I had never seen so many people. And their clothes were different, and even the shapes of their faces. Some were in fact dark-skinned. I was scared. I wished they would go away and leave me undisturbed. Some of them in fact did go away very soon. There were tales of young city mothers who took flight from the frightening silence of the countryside, from the superstitious dark, back into the world of pubs and chippies and street lights. The children, when they first came, were scared of drinking milk which they saw the cows 'pissing' into pails. They were lice-infested and bedclothes had to be burnt after they had slept in them. Their vocabulary was fruity and their accent incomprehensible to the monolingual population of Llŷn, who found English a contorted and tongue-twisting language at the best of times. There were children who slept under beds from force of habit and others who attacked their foster-parents both physically and mentally. The majority, however, adjusted. Some stayed on after the war. And became part of us. And learnt Welsh. And became indistinguishable, in time, from other human beings. As for me, I learnt English. My teachers were called Philip and Roger, and they stayed at the Post Office at Dinas where I went to school. Philip was old and dreamy. Roger was rough, rampaging and trampling all over my territory. As I grew into consciousness, I had learnt to fashion my own life in my own way. An only child, in a locality where children were widely scattered and more accustomed to the company of adults than to the company of each other, I created my own social order. The orchard, the laurels, the field, the den over the way where trees rose from a hidden dell into the open sky and were easily climbable, and the woods and parks of Madryn, and ultimately, Garn Fadryn itself, were all thickly populated with my creations, and they all behaved as I wanted them to. Philip and Roger did not, and that was something I had to learn to adjust to, like it or not.

Garn Fadryn dominates Llŷn. Wherever you go Y Garn rears its head over the blackthorn hedges, sometimes solid and squat, at other times and from other angles as graceful as Snowdon. Sometimes its summit seems an easy picnic journey on a fine afternoon, at other times a fair climber's challenge, with its purple slopes and its waterfalls of scree. From certain vantage points, it looks a much higher mountain than the twelve hundred feet allocated to it in the official guides.

To anyone brought up in Llŷn, Y Garn hovers eternally on the mind's horizons. To climb Y Garn was a statutory part of every holiday. Especially every summer holiday. To gather bilberries perhaps, from the low bushes that extend over the upper slopes. Or simply to chew thick sandwiches on Arthur's Table, looking down from the western side of the summit towards Rhiw and Aberdaron, and to follow ultimately the meandering path that lost itself in the broadleafed forest as it descended towards Madryn Castle.

There is no Madryn Castle now. It's a caravan site. One stone arch is the only remaining memory of the house that was a family seat for centuries and then for a time an agricultural college. The poets sang the praises of Madryn in the middle ages, and when the old society was shattered, and Royalist and Parliamentarian fought for domination, the Madryn family were committed Puritans, with Sir Thomas Madryn fighting in Cromwell's army. Then the estate fell into the hands of the nearby Rhydolion family. They too were Puritans. And after the Puritans' custom of naming their children after certain of the Christian virtues, 'Love' became incorporated into the family name. It was, by all accounts, an apt choice for the male members.

Although they were certainly wholehearted in their commitment to Parliament, and indeed to the Puritan cause, they do not appear to have been particularly Puritan in their outlook. They were a breed of romantic, colourful adventurers, the Love Jones Parrys, full of chivalrous gestures. Perhaps their most romantic connection of all was the Captain Love who went out with Lewis Jones to Patagonia in 1863, two years before the main group of settlers sailed in the *Mimosa* to establish their Welsh colony. Lewis Jones and Captain Love were shrewd public relations men, and less than accurate in their descriptions of the many blessings that the hapless colonists would find when they arrived in Patagonia. The trauma of discovering the truth about the South American pampas must have been earth-shattering for those desperate crofters and quarrymen and South Wales miners. Needless to say, Love himself did not venture there again, although he did defend their cause more than once in Parliament.

In terms of personality, there is no question that his father, universally known as 'The Old Sir Love', was the people's favourite. He was an eccentric philanthropist who struggled to communicate with his tenants in his own unorthodox version of the Welsh language, made Madryn a refuge for the unfortunate, was a quixotically generous patron of poets and writers, and used his position as a magistrate to ease the lot of many who had, in his judgement, been ill-used by fate. Cybi, poetically named after his birthplace of Llangybi, one of the historian-poets bred so prolifically in localities like these at the end of the last century and the beginning of this, describes him in his *Cymeriadau Hynod Sir Gaernarfon,* published in 1923. He shows in a way how some of the strong links of patronage and cultural autonomy that were so outstanding a feature of the relationships between the Court Poets of the fourteenth and fifteenth centuries and their patrons among the gentry, lived on in localities like this for a very long time. There lived in Chwilog, for example, at the end of the eighteenth century and the beginning of the nineteenth, a poet named John Thomas, claimed by my mother's family as an ancestor, Sion Wyn of Eifion. He was struck down by a crippling illness at the age of fourteen, and spent twenty-five years of the remainder of a long life – he died in 1859 at the age of seventy-three – entirely bedridden. Gradually, with great courage and iron will, he was able to rise from his bed for some hours each day into a kind of handcart he himself had invented. But he never recovered. His home, to all intents and purposes, was a wainscot-bed surrounded by books. He became widely read in a number of languages, and a poet of some distinction. 'Old Sir Love', it is said, owned his cottage, and the only rent he exacted was one poem a year. He too, it appears, provided the handcart, and many of the books.

From the foot of Y Garn, as I awoke in the morning, and drew the curtains in the bedroom, I would look up to the summit for the daily weather forecast. If Y Garn wore its cap, there was no holiday weather for me that day. And then, in the evening, even to a child's matter-of-factness, its purple silhouette, reflected in the millpond below our house, was an awesome sight. Pennant went to see Y Garn a hundred and fifty years ago:

> I took a ride about five miles inland to Carn Madryn, a lofty, rocky, insulated hill noted for having been a strong-hold of the sons of Owain Gwynedd, Roderick and Malgwyn, to whom this part of the country belonged. The bottom, sides and top, are fitted with cells, oblong, oval or circular, once thatched, or covered from the inclemency of the weather: many of them are pretty entire. The chieftains resided on the top; the people of the country, with their cattle, in times of invasion, occupied the sides and bottom. The whole summit is surrounded with a wall, still visible in many places. From the summit is an extensive view of the country, with the bay of Caernarvon on one side, and that of Cardigan on the other. Sarn Badrig is seen extending from Meirioneddshire, its dangerous length, nearly parallel to the shore of Llŷn. South Wales may be seen plainly, and in clear weather, Ireland; and in front the whole tract of Snowdonia exhibits a most magnificent and stupendous barrier . . .

And that is a continuing impression. A stronghold beyond the strongholds. The whole arrogant range of peaks that make Snowdonia a complete, impregnable defensive wall, seems so far away. And Yr Eifl and Y Garn rise in the middle of an entirely Welsh territory, undisputed rulers of the land.

And yet it's clear that these parts were vulnerable to attacks from the sea. The Vikings came, and then the Irish, and the old poets write of Garn Fadryn as a military strongpoint, a vantage place, an embattled outpost where soldiers are constantly on the lookout for the enemy. Sion Phylip, a sixteenth-century poet, writes of its hill fort in an englyn:

The throne of all Gwynedd 'tween Llŷn – and the sky
On a royal, green mountain,
Strong stonework tightly woven,
Immortal defence – Carnfadryn.

And the same poet is direct in his description of the guards who watch from that fort:

Scarred and battered those grey men – in clothes
Of rough broadcloth pattern,
Grave, silent, motionless men,
On a hill watching for treason.

And another poet, Huw Pennant, from the same period, writes of the watchers on Y Garn warning the whole area of the coming of any threatening ship over the horizon to the west.

The hill-fort is itself a witness to the dangers that surrounded those who lived at this end of the peninsula. It was originally built during the Iron Age but, like the more famous hill-village on Yr Eifl, it was no doubt inhabited much later than that, and possibly used spasmodically as a refuge far on into the Christian period, and even later than that if the poets' specific references are to be accepted as more than fantasy. Here, at the foot of Y Garn, I went to my second school. I remember little of Bryncroes school, other than that a horror of school dentists was generated there by the English phrase, 'Next child', shouted in English through the partition in the big schoolroom, and the fact that the teachers too spoke English, at least for official purposes. The only phrases I remember using myself were 'Yessir' and 'Snosir'; this seemed to be sufficient for my immediate purposes. I also realise in retrospect that, in common with many headmasters of the time, at their wits' end to know how to deal with lusty farmers' sons, unscholastic fourteen-year-olds dying to be up and doing on the farm, the *Sgŵl* at Bryncroes used the senior boys to dig his garden and grow his vegetables, and to occupy themselves in other ways about his domestic business. Although I don't recall learning anything in Bryncroes, the school, in retrospect, seems to have been peaceful and uneventful enough, a no-account interlude between the imaginative adventures of home and freedom. This could not be said of my second school. If the headmaster at Bryncroes dealt with the problem of educating growing boys without the help of any appropriate syllabus by making them dig his garden, the headmaster at Dinas believed in the rule of the rod. He would call the whole Junior school from behind its protective partition and pack us all into the front desks of the senior classroom. Then he would turn, open a glass-fronted cupboard behind him, and take out a stout stick, bow-bent from constant use. The intended victim was then called out to the front and told to hold out his hand. If he obeyed unquestioningly, he would be berated, lashed on the hands and sent back sobbing to his seat. But some of the bolder spirits would sometimes protest their innocence, or even try to defy their imminent doom by muttering some impertinence. If this happened, the headmaster would go berserk and chase his victim about the room, yelling and screaming, beating him all over with his stick – legs, buttocks and shoulders, until he subsided howling on the floor, or ran out of the door and disappeared for the remainder of the day. I remember one ghastly morning when we were called to the senior schoolroom and we all filed in, white-faced and silent. A parent was in there, an irate father who held his hat in his hands and stood, red-faced, facing the headmaster. He ran the local shop.

'It was one of your boys,' he was saying, 'and I want to see him punished.'

The headmaster strode among the desks, grabbed one of the older lads by the scruff of the neck and hauled him out to the front.

'This one, was it?' he snapped.

'Probably,' said the man. 'They're all the same. All hooligans. All thieves. You have no control over them at all.'

'No control!' The headmaster's high-pitched squeal silenced every movement, every mutter. 'I'll show you control. I'll show you how I deal with them.'

'It's your business, not mine,' said the man, putting his hat on his head, and walking out. 'Just deal with him, that's all.'

The beating the poor lad received that morning drew blood from his scampering legs and left him whimpering in a corner. We returned to our classroom ashen-faced and shaking. Our teacher, a small, bespectacled woman, would be almost as upset as we were by these rituals and very little would be done in the junior classroom for the remainder of the day, what with a sporadically weeping teacher and a petrified class. My father, as the parish priest, was chairman of the school's 'managers' as they were called, but he didn't seem to be able to achieve anything in the way of reform other than my eventual removal to Morfa Nefyn. No doubt some normal education took place at Dinas, but I recall none of it, except that we wrote with slate pencils on slate slabs and spat on them to remove the writing. School meals were also introduced while I was there, and they consisted of unvarying cawl, made mainly with swedes and one huge chunk of mutton. But my world in Dinas was not the world of school. As others have testified in previous generations, the Council School in rural Wales, especially if it was a Church, or National, School, was often both alien and barbaric. I don't remember any overt linguistic repression in Dinas – I think Welsh was more or less accepted – but its barbarism was endemic and life at school for a small boy was something to be endured. My real world, my imaginative world, existed outside its walls.

Philip and Roger, whom I cannot remember having been in school at all, had to be fitted in to this world. Communication does not seem, in retrospect, to have been particularly difficult, although they certainly spoke no Welsh, and my English was minimal. Gradually we built up an all-purpose vocabulary which served our purpose, some English words, some Welsh words, many complex gestures. I never learnt anything of their background; their parents, as far as I know, never ventured into Llŷn. Later, when we used to go to Liverpool for our annual holiday in early September, to shop at Lewis's, to visit the funfair at New Brighton on the ferry from Pierhead, to watch Everton play at Goodison Park, and to enter the dark cave of Liverpool cathedral on Sunday mornings, I became familiar with Philip and Roger's city. But I never met them there, and they were never referred to. I got to know Liverpool well, for my parents, although in many ways conventional, were also prepared to take risks. And I would wander the streets of Liverpool alone, while my mother shopped at Lewis's. We would meet for lunch at Cooper's. Cooper's was exciting because it was below street level and smelt of coffee, and because there were musicians there, playing their instruments while we ate. The street was exciting because it contained the News Theatre, a cinema where there was no feature film, only Pathé News, and cartoons, and ten-minute comedies, and serials. There were pink and green and mauve lights, and ice-cream girls. It was my spiritual home in the city. But Philip and Roger belonged in Llŷn.

I took them eventually to the one place that mattered more even than my fields and dens around the house. Down the steep hill, almost under the mountain, was the water mill. There were ghosts by the millpond.

The road, as it came down from 'The Rectory', crossed a stream over what almost amounted to a viaduct, a towering wall at the front of which was a tunnel that allowed the stream to squeeze through. And down there, in the shadow of the wall, was the mill. And behind the mill were twin millponds, and beyond the millponds, the mountain. At Felin Fadryn, although regular milling for the locality had ceased, they did a limited amount of milling once a week for themselves and for certain favoured customers like the college at Madryn Castle. I would go down on such mornings and climb up rickety wooden ladders through trapdoors in two wooden floors until I arrived at the millpond level, the waterwheel level, the level where the huge iron axle came through the stone wall and slowly turned the millstones in the belly of the building. Everything up there was a flurry of fine dust and chaff and lost ears of corn and rejected, rusty cogs, and the grinding sound of pulleys and chains, and behind it all the massive ancient stones turning and turning. Once the lurching machinery had begun to operate, I would run pellmell down the wooden ladders and around the overgrown paths to the smaller of the two ponds. From there

I could see the water pouring down from the higher pond through the open floodgate to the lower pond, and then in a crystal waterfall from there onto the great rungs of the wheel. The wheel would start to move very reluctantly, stiffly. And then it gradually accelerated, until it and the water and the still pictures of mountain, trees and buildings in the two dark ponds came to form a smooth eternal rhythm. I would stand there, lost for minutes, perhaps hours, until Huw Owen's wife, Leusa, who died young and went to lie in the churchyard in Dinas, called me into the house for a glass of warm milk. Then back to the mill. Back up the wooden ladders. By now, the whole building was groaning and rattling and straining to contain the throb and thump of the machinery. Up above, there were names and dates and messages all over the walls, going back to 1896 when someone had drawn a heart with an arrow through it, and the letters L and E beside the date. I took Philip and Roger to Felin Fadryn. But not immediately. And I took them up the mountain itself, a mountain that had previously been reserved for picnics with my mother, or by myself.

It was a sparkling day when I first took Philip and Roger up there. Up above the woods, there was a light breeze playing in our hair, but as we climbed higher and looked down, a heat haze lay still and low over Hell's Mouth, which looked innocuous enough, and the rocks of Garn Fach, rising behind us, almost reflected the heat of the sun. On either side of the path that twists and turns and doubles back on itself as it climbs towards the scree, there is always in the spring a profusion of wild flowers, often half-hidden in the bilberry clumps, where the tiny red unripe fruit, almost invisible from a distance, but a huge rash all over the stunted green bushes when one stops and bends towards them, give promise of a great purple blackness all over these slopes in late June.

From time to time on the way up, the huge rocks that were left here some time during the Ice Age to gather moss and fennel, reveal between them the slit entrance of a cave. And we struggled through the uneven bracken and peered in. Garn Fadryn was once a paradise for foxes, and I told them of the time when I hunted them. Not with smart horses and dogs and red coats, but in the company of the keeper at Nanhoron, and with a tiny white terrier that was brave and foolhardy enough to venture into the darkness of any underground cavern. We almost lost him once. We waited for hours, like relatives at a pithead, until the dusk gathered, listening for the echo of a bark from the depths and imagining its sound over and over. Eventually, as it happened, the dog surfaced a full quarter of a mile away, and ran proudly towards us, the blood on his jaws a betrayal of a secret battle somewhere in the corridors below. We didn't see any foxes, but John Jones, Myrddin Fardd – the author of *Enwau Lleoedd* ('Place Names') – says, hopefully, that 'fox' is the original meaning of the word 'madryn'.

Finally, we breasted the rise and came upon the wide open shoulder of the mountain, heathland and bog, and on the far side of it, in the shadow of the summit itself, the ruined streets of the hill-fort.

This fort is among the largest in Wales, and this one and its partner a few miles away on Garn Boduan were earlier examples than Tre'r Ceiri on Yr Eifl. The first fortification extends over twelve acres, with a dry stone wall around it – and various round dwellings gathered in groups inside. Then there was a later, larger extension, which covered twenty-five acres. We wandered among the ruins, gingerly feeling our way forward as we went. The moss and plant growth of centuries had created a false floor, and we were liable to plunge some feet into a genuine hollow between the piled-up stones. And from that hollow, insulation from the wind and the cold of these high places was complete.

And then we walked up to the summit. There, spread out before us, was the strip of green pasture that was my guarantee of identity. And beyond it the sea. Stretching across to the dully discernible shadow of Patricia's Wicklow Hills.

On that green strip are the patterned fields, closed in behind their high hedges, blackthorn and whitethorn, gorse and bracken and packed earth. And here and there, in a line across from Yr Eifl, in their tiny square graveyards, with ash and elder to protect them, stand the grey churches of Llŷn, ancient, hidden, built very often on holy places that go back through the druidical period to the Neolithic dark.

Churches naturally featured in my life; and churches, to me, were small, flickering places, lit by paraffin lamps and full of staccato harmonium music in the pale evening.

Ceidio church stands on rising ground, and from that hillock one can look back along the Pilgrims' Way, through Nefyn and Pistyll to Clynnog in one direction, and then if one turns one's head westwards, to Llandudwen, Penllech, Llangwnadl, and finally Aberdaron.

Suddenly, as you round a bend in the narrow lane, it appears, framed in an arch of overhanging branches, high on a knoll above you, like a stag sniffing the wind in its own territory. Its unexpected double belfry is like a set of great antlers that punch the sky.

Ceidio's positioning is unusual among the churches of Llŷn. Most of them hide and nestle in hollows. But for all its forthright position, very little is known of its past. Ceidio, it seems, was a follower of Beuno, and so the original church was part of the first wave of evangelisation that swept across Llŷn. And although the church is something of an empty shell today, yet there are still marks of dignity here. The building itself is simple, unadorned, and the east window, which is intact, shows the crucifixion in monochrome silhouette, the white light striking against the dark, leaden framework with stark effect.

The road from Ceidio to Llandudwen takes you to the crossroads, where you turn your backs again on Nefyn, and walk towards the south-west. On the land of Cefn Leisiog farm, a primitive radar station was built during the war, with huge wooden pylons, thick and clumsy, interspersed with more elegant, experimental metal ones, that were taller and thinner. The litter remains today. Concrete foundations, twisted metal structures, even ancient barbed wire entanglements, the remnants of a non-existent war. Past the fields and the farm the road comes to a sharp left turn. Up another shaded, narrow lane, and left again. You arrive at the very foot of Y Garn, and it rears its head above you darkly. Before long you come to a long shaded lane leading sharply down to the left. As you walk down its grassgrown gravel towards Llandudwen Church, you look directly towards Nefyn and Porthdinllaen. Hidden in the woods on the southerly slopes of Garn Boduan is yet another Iron Age fort.

Llandudwen is a world in itself. Surrounded by a small, square cemetery, entered by a lych-gate that is at least as old as the church. One approaches the lych-gate along a narrow walk, shadowed once again by stone walls. A fairly recent iron gate opens onto this path, and a mounting-block stands near by, where the worshippers dismounted from their horses, and no doubt left them tethered by the gate, as they went on into the church. The churchyard is sheltered and as calm and consecrated as a cathedral close. Immediately above, Y Garn is again obtrusive. The church is tiny, and you have to bow your head to step in through the low door. Most of this present building dates from the twelfth century, although a church was built here almost certainly as early as the seventh century by an anchorite called Tudwen. As with many of the early Christians, however little known outside their locality today, Tudwen was known as one who possessed healing powers and, difficult to identify by now, but still there, St Tudwen's Well lies a field's length away from the churchyard. Myrddin knew all about it, and rated it highly:

> many travelled to it long distances; they threw money and new pins into it . . . for its waters were considered effective to counter diseases of the eye, rheumatism and Epilepsy, that is, some sort of fainting fits . . .

Myrddin also claimed that Ffynnon Tudwen was a favourite spot to conduct clandestine marriages, and that many also wished to be baptised by its waters. Its inaccessibility, even in terms of those pedestrian days, meant that it did not come to national fame, as did Ffynnon Fair and Ffynnon Beuno, but its waters were clearly regarded as possessing more than ordinary power.

Inside the church, it is dark. The windows are small, deep-set within massive walls, and their sloping sills give them an air of fortification. What attracts the eye at once is the unexpectedly sharp colouring of the stained glass in the small, oblong east windows. There, in red and blue and gold – the staple colours of pre-Renaissance religious art (although the blue is more positive than one usually sees) – are all the universal symbols of Christianity: the Greek letters XP, Christos Rex, and the letters Alpha and Omega on twin windows, and IHS. The colours from these windows throw shifting, blended light all around the east end of the church, especially in the morning; and, in a certain combination of time and sunlight, a direct reversed image is thrown on the cool cave in the stone wall where the bread and wine were kept centuries ago.

This was one of my father's churches. He would bustle in and clean it and whitewash it and make the place presentable for the few who came. I would often wander in while he was engaged in his scrubbing and whitewashing, and it was then that most of my early education took place. He would pontificate, about kings and queens of ancient times, about soldier-heroes, even about contemporary events. I would sit and listen until, bored by immobility, I would wander out to create some other world, a world of sailing ships or trenches or Sherwood Forest among the trees and gravestones of the churchyard. My father was, in fact, a stickler for the appearance of his churches. He found this one a pigsty, and transformed it. Gave it back its coolness, its bare stones, its age. And at thanksgiving, the place was full. Chapel people came, and people I never knew. They walked, with torches, from Dinas and even Llaniestyn, because the thanksgiving date would be a late one, and winter would be drawing in.

They sat bolt upright, and put their hats on the seats beside them. And paraffin lamps threw great shadows over their faces. The big, open faces of Llŷn, earth faces, with faraway eyes, the men's red necks overflowing their hard white collars, and their wide fingers gripping their hymnbooks. The women were dark, solid, black eyes deep and secretive. My father's shadow was huge from the pulpit on the flickering wall. And while they put their heads in their hands and prayed, I looked at the windows and remembered them in sunlight, Alpha and Omega, Christos Rex, the eternal symbols opening out onto a world I had never seen.

Above us, as we made our way out, on moonlit nights the mountain would seem vast. And always, night and day, it was unyieldingly there. And so the road winds through Dinas. It holds no fond memories. And then over the top of Rhosddu and down into Sarn Mellteyrn, a kind of sub-capital for this part of Llŷn – more, certainly, than just a village. And yet its antecedents seem uncertain. Rhabanian's *Archaeologia Lleyniensis* moves rapidly into the field of fantasy as it talks about it, and Myrddin's *Enwau Lleoedd* is undecided whether the name is derived from the Welsh 'byllt heyrn', iron bars, from an original dedication to St Peter ad Vinculis, or whether a Celtic saint named Mellteyrn established a community here. Whatever the truth of the matter, Sarn, lying in its hollow, is the natural centre of Llŷn; roads lead down into it from all directions, and it was an important stopping-off point for the staging-horses. And an initial junction for drovers too.

The road moves through it and becomes windswept as it leads along the foot of Mynydd Cefnamlwch towards the sea. In the lee of the mountain, but out of our sight, stands the 'plas'. And the family who lived there, like the Madryn family, played its part in Welsh history. Griffith was the family name, and it was from here that Madame Griffith came – she played a substantial part in Hywel Harries's eighteenth-century attempt to set up a mixed monastic community at Trefeca. The family claimed descent from one of the most famous of the early Welsh princes, Rhys ap Tewdwr. And they were, for a long time, Welsh in speech and spirit, although it appears, from his censorious references to them, that they were not so when Myrddin was writing his books about Caernarfonshire.

Before the road reaches a junction that takes you left along the coast towards Llangwnadl, there is a cromlech, standing up, unfenced, in the centre of a field.

Garn Fadryn now seems distant as we look across at it from this cromlech, perfect in its formation, but unattended and seemingly disregarded. The cromlech is situated in the parish of Penllech, and the little church of Penllech, anonymous among farm buildings on our right, is once more placed in its square plot of land and surrounded by stone walls, almost aggressively simple and ascetic. It would be easy to pass by and think it was no more than a well-built barn. Like Ceidio, Llandudwen, Pistyll, Garngiwch, Llanaelhaearn, dotted around the landscape with such prodigality, the extreme simplicity of these buildings, and the dignity built into that simplicity, has a telling effect. In each one separately, one feels an individual character, a calm assumption of its right to be there. But when one stands back and considers all this proliferation of individual witness, all this multiplication of religious experience, one is struck with a sense of awe.

Penllech, like many similar churches, housed a local day-school, run by the bellringer, before there was any other kind of day-school in the locality. Bad though some of these day-schools were, others made significant contributions, notably Eben Fardd's school in Clynnog. And they filled gaps, more or less inadequately, until eventually, haltingly, a state system of schooling took over. Nor was that always an improvement. The history of this school at Penllech contains a cameo of the kind of thing that was achieved in a muddled way, the kind of salvage operation that such schools could sometimes perform. One of those who obtained his first schooling at Penllech, in the sixteenth century, was a boy named Henry Rowlands from the neighbouring parish of Sarn Mellteyrn. He went on from here to New College, Oxford, entered the church, was made Dean of Bangor in 1593 and Bishop of Bangor in 1598. When he died in 1616, he left substantial sums of money, not only to establish scholarships for Welsh boys at Jesus College, Oxford, but also to found a local grammar school at Botwnog. That school still flourishes, and is now the comprehensive school for all the villages at the far end of Llŷn, and perhaps the most naturally Welsh-speaking of all the secondary schools of Wales.

Now it becomes increasingly obvious that the road has left the warm, green, sheltered localities that cluster around Garn Fadryn, and has entered a different landscape. This area is rugged, windswept, bleak. Everything is more harsh, more open. And the sea beats audibly on the shore. This locality gives credence to the belief that Llŷn is not in any real sense a peninsula, but an island.

And yet the church at Llangwnadl, when the road turns down towards it within a mile or two, has found shelter. It stands, like Pistyll and Llandudwen, in its grove of trees, a low building, with a superb modern wrought-iron gate leading into the churchyard. The words, 'Tŷ Dduw' (House of God), are worked into the gate.

The church has a triple nave, and the complexity of arches, the ornamented stonework around the windows, on the font, and on the supporting pillars, all suggest a small but significant departure from the stern simplicity of the other churches. Apart from the fact that Llangwnadl developed into an important resting-place for pilgrims, a last halt before reaching Aberdaron, there is another reason for the difference; and the reason throws a new shaft of light onto the reality of the Age of the Saints in Llŷn.

On one of the pillars, near the east end, are ornamentally carved the words *Hic iacet Gwynhoydyl*. Gwynhoedl, as he is usually known, was probably neither a monk nor a priest, but a local chief of some status and wealth who gave the land for the first church to be built here to house the new Christian community. And the fact that he took the community under his wing naturally ensured that it flourished. And so, his reward was the perpetuation of his name. If he did not attain sainthood, he achieved immortality, a reasonable return for generosity.

We know by now that the link between the secular power and the new spiritual crusade was a vital factor in the Christianising of Wales. The coming of Christianity not only effected people's beliefs and form of worship. It transformed the whole structure of society. During the Age of the Saints, during the fifth, sixth and early seventh centuries, a civilized society was built up in Wales; the foundations of medieval chivalry were laid; barbarism was temporarily left behind. Just as Maelgwn's support was vital to the establishment of Deiniol's 'clâs' in Bangor, and Gwyddneint to Beuno's at Clynnog, so the commitment of local landowners like Gwynhoedl was equally vital in the smaller localities. And it was apt that when the third part of the church was built in 1520, three centuries after the oldest parts of the building, and the stone carver recorded the fact on a pillar *Hic ecclesia edificator est in anno domini 1520*, he also took the trouble to record on a neighbouring pillar that the man who started it all is buried here, in the church he made possible.

This road may end in Llangwnadl or on Bardsey itself, but there was also another pilgrims' way running through Llŷn, on the other side of Garn Fadryn, and meeting this one at Aberdaron. Those travelling to Bardsey from the north would follow the first route. But those travelling from the south might well come by sea to Pwllheli, and take a different path. This path will eventually bring them to the church at Llanengan. This is said to be the oldest extant complete building in Llŷn, and there is a very strong tradition that the rood screen that now adorns the church had been brought here from the abbey in Bardsey itself. Along the south side of Llŷn, after leaving Abersoch, the roads weave among tiny knolls past this church until they emerge in the openness of Hell's Mouth. Hell's Mouth can live up to its name in winter, but I remember it as a vast, empty summer beach to which we walked across footpaths and farmyards when we lived at the dower house of Gelliwig. When I was small, my mother would be the guide on all such expeditions as this, walking or cycling. After we moved to Gelliwig she was the universal provider and still thoroughly necessary, as we dragged a gaggle of friends in tow, often friends from my boarding-school who had cadged a summer holiday. She carried the tea, the sweaters, and the only timepiece, but often we all stayed there, on the beach and footpaths, until the late summer dark caught up with us and we had to stumble our way home through muddy ditches and arrive bespattered with cowpats. No tourist had penetrated as far as Hell's Mouth at that time. We owned it all. But at one end of it, the Aberdaron end, there was a group of fishermen's huts and above these huts a cave which was reputed to be the sea-entrance to a smugglers' tunnel that led to the little manor-house of Plas-yn-Rhiw, well hidden among the trees above. We peered into the dark opening of the cave, but never penetrated far, and looked wonderingly up the steep slope towards the hidden smugglers' stronghold instead. As it happened, the contemporary owners of Plas-yn-Rhiw were at least as romantic as any smuggler's tale could have been. I did meet them as a small boy at my mother's apron-strings when she was invited to some charity tea-party there. My impression was of an old, cold house with a smoking choking fire. We sat around tables loaded with scones and three old ladies poured tea from huge teapots and pressed cakes and strawberry jam on all and sundry while they talked incessantly in English and poked and cursed the unwilling blaze. They redeemed themselves, however, by serving me ginger beer from a stone bottle, and giving me a pewter mug to drink it out of. If anything was needed to prove that Plas-yn-Rhiw was a smuggler's stronghold, this was certainly sufficient. But how to conceive of these prattling ancient women as daring smugglers was another matter. I left Plas-yn-Rhiw well-fed and bewildered, but soon put them out of my mind. It was some years before I came to realise the true gallantry that underlay these three sisters' occupancy of Plas-yn-Rhiw. And their true eccentricity. The Keatings, as they were known throughout Llŷn, were English by birth, but of Irish extraction. I do not know how they came by Plas-yn-Rhiw, but they were reputedly fabulously rich, owning much property in Nottingham and elsewhere. I came to know them during subsequent pastoral visits at my father's elbow and began to distinguish one from the other. Eileen was the eldest, the mother-figure who cared for the others, and seemed to have done so since girlhood. Honor, the middle sister, was the one who had succeeded in society. Tall and elegant, calm and composed beside the fussy chatter of her sisters, she didn't seem to belong. Honor was looked up to, allowed to retire to her room to 'write'; she had been awarded the OBE for some humanitarian work during the Depression; predictably, she painted water-colours. Lorna, the youngest, was the family handyman, the gardener, the one who was indulged. They loved Llŷn, its naturalness and its green peace, with an inordinate passion. They devoted all their energies and many of their financial resources to maintaining it as it was. They bought stretches of coastline and ensured that caravan sites would not spawn upon it; they placed stringent conditions on the tenants of their farms and cottages; it was said that their resistance and their stubborn refusal to sell land was mainly responsible for the failure of the Central Electricity Generating Board, or whatever its equivalent then was, to establish a nuclear power station at Edern, a stone's throw away from my grandmother's house in Morfa Nefyn. And they certainly prevented the erection of a radar tracking station on Mynydd Anelog, at the wild and windswept furthest promontory of Llŷn, looking out on Bardsey Island. In all this, in the face of press campaigns and public and private harassment, they remained totally implacable. They were certainly eccentric – on the day their mother died, my father arrived there to find the old lady's body propped up in a wicker basket-chair, in the window, taking the sun. But their priorities were clear and unchanging, cultured and civilized to the end. When Lorna broke her leg, Eileen, old and arthritic, travelled daily by bus to the hospital in Bangor to bring her her favourite delicacies; the return trip took her all day, and she kept it up for weeks. There was, of course, a negative side to their comprehensive pantheism. When they eventually buried their mother, they did so in the tiny churchyard of Llanfaelrhys, looking out to sea, under a rough boulder. When a farmer tried to build a barn between the grave and the western horizon, they instantly instructed their faithful solicitor to prevent him doing so – it interfered with the old lady's view of the sea. There were many who regarded them as wrong-headed, obscurantist, even downright silly. Lorna, unable to cope once she was left alone, died lonely and confused only a few years ago; she didn't know me when I visited her in her geriatric hospice. But she could have died easy. The Keatings had passed on their beautiful house and all their wide and varied acres to the nation, tied up and conserved till Kingdom Come. Theirs was a sensitivity beyond the wisdom of utilitarian politics. As we walked our footpaths home from Hell's Mouth, through gorse and bracken, scaring the rabbits beneath our feet, eating the wild strawberries as we went, we might have spared a thought for the mad old ladies in Plas-yn-Rhiw. It was they who understood the basis of our summer freedom and our summer joy.

The village of Llanengan is situated in the complex of lanes and hillocks around Hell's Mouth. But the church, sheltered as it is, also looks out across level ground at the inevitable distant view of Garn Fadryn, and the low-lying land between here and Botwnnog. The interior is light and open, and the whole building breathes a serenity. It is far bigger than most of the churches in Llŷn, and apart from its screen, where the delicate fifteenth-century carving contrasts with the crudely-fashioned monks' seats, constructed a century or more earlier, there are other indications of its age and importance. It is said that the chest, reminiscent of Beuno's chest at Clynnog, also came from Bardsey, and this too had three locks as a guarantee of its security.

The building, probably a combination of eleventh and twelfth-century work, is as imposing as it is for reasons similar to those surrounding the nature of Llangwnadl. The first church at Llanengan was established by a man named Einion or Eingion, sometimes known as 'King Einion'. Elsewhere, he is referred to as the Dean of Llŷn, and Myrddin traces his descent from Cunedda, thus making him of the same status and generation as Maelgwn Gwynedd and Seiriol. He was clearly a local chieftain of some importance, and, apart from founding a church at Llanengan, he also supported Cadfan in establishing the first priory on Bardsey.

These roads, five, six, seven centuries ago, were alive with pilgrims, caught up in the mysterious attraction of Bardsey. And that in its turn was simply symbolic of the tremendous activity that had taken place, five, six, seven centuries before that, throughout the peninsula. From Clynnog up to Llanaelhaearn, down through Pistyll to Nefyn and on, there is hardly a square mile that doesn't possess concrete evidence of the work of some Christian or group of Christians in early days. Church after church, built some time between the twelfth and fifteenth centuries, on sites consecrated earlier by the efforts of the pioneers themselves. And these same localities have an underlying web of religious activity that is earlier still. There are thirty-one British camps or hill-forts in Llŷn, twelve cromlechs and countless standing stones, bearing witness to an area where the sense of the numinous and an awareness of eternal realities has been intense and compulsive since the beginning of human habitation.

Stand on the summit of Garn Fadryn, as I did with Philip and Roger, with my mother on blackberrying expeditions, with Patricia, with alien English friends, often alone, and look to the north-east. You can see a line of hill-forts stretching back from the one at your feet, through the camp lurking in its grove of trees on Garn Boduan, to the great encampment on Yr Eifl, and on again through Anglesey to Holyhead. And as you stand there, you can also see the tight pattern of Christian influence, a far older pattern than the ordered geometry of the tidy fields. Pistyll, Nefyn, Ceidio, Llandudwen, Llaniestyn, Penllech, Llangwnadl, on the one side, and Llanbedrog, Llanengan, Llanfaelrhys and Rhiw on the other, each one in its plot of land, enclaves of belief and civilization in a world of barbarism. And that, of course, is how it still is. Come down from Y Garn, and go into any one of them, and it isn't difficult to feel how certain acres of land, over the centuries, begin to wear a cloak of sanctity, take on something of the life that has been lived in and around them. The Keatings understood this. Many who have lived here for generations know little about any of it, and care less. Others assume things will go on much as before, without any effort on their part. Others again can't wait for it all to change, for the tide of commercial know-how to sweep over Llŷn – lively seaside activities, entertainments, camp-sites equipped with hot water and toilets and kiddies' playgrounds. What use, in the end, are all these barren wild places, these damp churches, these dead-and-alive villages? As for me, when I was a child, churches and churchyards were homely places, warm and acceptable and lived-in, not in any way strange or otherworldly or dead-and-alive. I made them into theatres, acted plays in them, made great speeches from their pulpits, discovered the beauty of language in huge, damp-stained Bibles, and lay in the sun on warm tombstones, dreaming of the great events my father had called up out of the past. Many years later, when my father's body lay in its coffin in a church in Anglesey, I sat there late into the night and spoke to it; I strolled around the chancel, leaning on the bier, berating my father for getting himself killed in an unnecessary accident. It was a homely and natural feeling, very like those talks in Llandudwen many years before, except that he was, for once, silent.

# IV

All the time, wherever we moved within our narrow world, Nefyn was there. My grandmother's house was halfway between Nefyn and Morfa Nefyn. Exactly halfway. It was still the custom for seemly families from the North of England to visit Nefyn regularly every summer, some for as long as a month, others for a fortnight, staying always at the same house, paying for full board and lodging, occupying the best rooms, while my grandmother and her neighbours lived in the back and slept in the rambling attics. It was a period when tourism still had a human face.

Nowadays, things have suffered sea-changes. During the fifties and sixties Nefyn was still full of tourists, and the native population retreated all summer long to caravans and shacks at the bottom of the garden, and left the invaders to live in their houses. Subsequently tourists came to occupy houses, not to be boarded and served and cossetted. And instead of walking the village lanes and patronising the boatmen and attending the summer concerts in the village hall, built at the height of tourist prosperity, they hustled along the coastal roads, chasing the unusual and the picturesque; and the face of tourism assumed a smooth, impersonal mask. Now, they don't even occupy the houses – they simply drive through, caravanned and tented, and stare through car windows at the world around them.

Much of my summer life was spent in and on the sea. The bay at Nefyn is spectacular, enclosed on the north by the rocky precipices of Yr Eifl, as it plunges into the sea beyond Nant Gwrtheyrn, and on the south by the smaller, grass-covered headland that separates it from the wilder, more open bay of Porthdinllaen. We would sometimes climb over the headland to the stonier climate of 'Morfa', and trudge along that wide beach, past the narrow road that used to bring the stagecoach and the Royal Mail down to the inn at Tŷ Coch, and as far as Tŷ Coch itself. But that was not our objective. We would clamber past the old coachway inn, and negotiate the rocky path that snakes on towards the tip of the headland. And it was here, if we looked carefully, that we could see all around us the evidence of Porthdinllaen's shipbuilding days. It is still there. Rust-encrusted rings lie embedded in rock; the remains of old slipways, ancient anchors half-buried in the shale of the cliffside. We would go on past them until we came upon our tiny cove, a lost sheltered inlet before the jutting headland faced the open sea. Here the Porthdinllaen lifeboat was situated, and here we would lie on hot summer afternoons, hidden from the world, and swim away the sand and sweat of our long trudge from Nefyn.

My father used to tell of the power of the uncoiling braking-cable when the boat slid out of its stone house and thundered down the slipway into the sea, and described how he saw a lifeboatman's foot taken clean off on one occasion as it was caught inside the lethally tightening coil. I used to watch, fascinated, each time we went there to see the launching, and wished I were on board, snug in yellow oilskins, heroic in the storm. I never went. The lifeboat was an unattainable dream.

Nevertheless, I did go to sea. One of my earliest vivid memories is of sitting in the bottom of a swinging boat, eating periwinkles with a pin, the wooden seat above my head, and a pair of solid, sea-booted legs blocking my view. I had gone out fishing with my father on one of the large, open boats that still plied out of Nefyn for the famous herring. But more often for mackerel and whiting. A sudden storm had blown up, and we were riding it out. I was too young to be aware of danger, and familiar enough with the sea not to be afraid. I sat up and ate my periwinkles. It was one of many occasions when I went out with the fishermen. As I grew older, I would go by myself, and there were occasions of high excitement when we stayed overnight and came back with the dawn towards Nefyn headland, often drifting the last fifty yards through glassy water onto a silent, deserted beach. That beach would not have been deserted at the turn of the century. It was only a year or so ago that I sat on the high cliffs above Nefyn beach with John Parry. John Parry was over a hundred years old at the time, and as we sat there and talked, he pointed out, one by one, the schooners and four-masters that used to lie out there many years. He named and counted twenty-six ships that he had seen anchored simultaneously in the bay when he, as a ship's carpenter, went from ship to ship looking for work. Not many went to sea in my generation. John Parry was looking at a lost world.

But the power of the sea was driven home to us clearly enough. There was an occasion when I was employed to take an elderly couple from my grandmother's house out for a row in the bay. I went out further than my normal sheltered paddling area, and could see the waves freshening, and the white-capped breakers running before the wind in the distance. Time after time, the dangers of drifting in the direction of Black Rock and Pistyll, at the foot of Yr Eifl, had been impressed upon me. There, the treacherous currents and jagged rocks had spelt disaster for many boats. It was only a week or so since a sailing boat, with two lads from Nefyn on board, lads I knew vaguely, had drifted that way, capsized, and the two were never seen again. I sculled the boat laboriously around, and started to pull shorewards. But I wasn't strong, and I can still feel the panic setting in as I glanced sideways and saw that not only were we getting no nearer the shore, but we were drifting significantly towards Pistyll. I pulled and sweated and died inwardly, until I finally managed to drag the boat inshore, a long way from the boatmen's huts, but far enough from Pistyll. The elderly couple simply wondered why I had grounded them so unexpectedly in the wrong place.

We were not unaware of the dangers of the sea, but they rarely impinged directly on our consciousness. The war impinged even less. There were certainly concrete road-blocks at the top of the winding road that led down to the sea, mines were washed up on shore, and trenches were dug on the headland, soon to be overgrown and used only by lovers on summer evenings, but it was all, for us, a distant fantasy. Which was more than the lovers were. After I went to Morfa Nefyn School, I made friends there, and looked forward more and more to my summers, spent either with my grandmother in a hut and a tent, both balanced precariously on the cliffside above Nefyn beach. As tourism began to spread inland, our house in Dinas became a desirable residence and so we abandoned it for some weeks in the summer while it was occupied by the English. My father built the hut in Nefyn for us to live in and acquired an old Army bell-tent from somewhere and erected it nearby. This was to be our summer home during my late childhood and adolescence. I loved it, and after I had gone away to school I brought friends there to stay. And one of our entertainments was to spy on the lovers, writhing in the trenches on the headland, panting and entwined and blissfully unaware of the entranced eyes of growing boys, not quite certain of what was afoot, but feeling the excitement of hot kisses in the summer dusk and the pale whiteness of bare limbs. On rainy days we would sit in the tent and imagine we were in a ship at sea. The raindrops would batter the canvas, gradually staining it with a spreading dampness, and we would hear the wind whistling through the spray far below. My English friends would teach me things, card games and bad language and stories about sex. But the sea was mine, and the roaring wind, and I could see the questions in their frightened eyes when a thunderstorm broke over our stockade in the dead of night and the rain dripped through the sodden roof. But in all this there was no sense of war. The boatmen and the fishermen, of course, were older – or younger – than they would normally be. Deaths at sea were vaguely reported from time to time, and there was talk of convoys and 'The Blackout'. But as we had known nothing different, it all seemed natural enough. My uncle John had closed his little barber's shop and gone to war, and, for a time, guarded German prisoners in a cold camp at Lanark, commanded, he claimed, by a mad Scots major in a kilt. And he brought me cap-badges and buttons of many regiments when he came home on leave.

In Nefyn too there was a camp. An Italian camp. I passed it, unmoved and not greatly curious, every time I rode my bike from Morfa to Nefyn, and watched those men drifting around behind high fences. It was part of the landscape. It didn't seem particularly strange. And then we had our own spy scare. After Lord Haw-Haw had started referring to the Welsh coast in his broadcasts. One notable night, he began to talk of Bodfean Woods as a possible hiding-place for an invading army, and of the suitability of Porthdinllaen beach for landing-craft. I have no idea at what time of day Lord Haw-Haw used to broadcast, but I know that I was in my grandmother's house and very much awake when this broadcast came through. My Uncle Griff was there, and we heard the voice coming from the cabinet radio on stilts that stood in the corner. The reaction was electric. And it was electric throughout the whole village. I went on my bike to look at Bodfean Woods, but didn't dare venture over the hedge. That potential hiding-place of Germans was to remain for years a place to pass rapidly and warily, especially in the dark. At one time, soon after he was married, my Uncle Griff lived in the woods. He worked as a gardener in the big house, Plas Boduan, and lived in a cottage along a rambling lane, deep in the dark shadows. I would cycle there, for he and his young wife Gwyneth, and their rapidly growing houseful of children, represented a different way of life.

I found in Griff's presence and in Griff's house a sense of daring, a kind of almost disreputable excitement, that I never sensed elsewhere. In a family that was much concerned with respectability, the forbidden excitements of Drink and Sex were clearly present in Griff's life. He was known to be fond of his pint. But to actually frequent the 'Sportsman' in Nefyn or the 'Bryncynan Arms' in Morfa was to have signed at least a provisional contract with the devil, exacerbated by the fact that he never went to church or chapel, regarding the whole thing as humbug. And then, in his thirties, while working as a general gardener/ handyman at the Cecil Hotel in Morfa Nefyn, he had fallen in love with a young girl from Rhosgadfan, far away near Caernarfon, who was also working there. He married her when she was, I think, nineteen. Griff and Gwyneth would actually make public demonstrations of their affection – something that was totally unfamiliar to me, and something that was no doubt frowned on by the remainder of the family. But Griff was never one to show great concern for family sensibilities. Blunt, witty, full of puzzles, ideas, and disreputable habits, I regarded him with something approaching adoration. And so, when this dark girl came to my grandmother's house, and stroked Griff's thick black hair while he lay on the living-room sofa, it was a curious, but acceptable phenomenon. The business was clearly serious. And it was, in some way, beautiful. When they married and moved around from house to house in the neighbourhood, before taking root on a council estate in Morfa Nefyn, I used to visit them often. They had five children, and I took turns at nursing each one of them, and I taught them football, and, all the time, watched Griff. He had a small, lively mongrel, a huge ironclad bike, and a pipe. And he took me poaching. In the shivering dark, we would creep along the hedgerows, waiting until an absence of human beings could be combined with a potshot at a rabbit. Then one shot, and over into the field we would go, scoop up the soft, warm booty, and away again into the dusk. Then we would sit and rest, in the shelter of the high Llŷn hedges, and he would tell me things. How to tie knots. How to make mice out of handkerchiefs. How to pack a pipe so that it would burn steadily, but not too fast. How to shoot. Gradually, I would be allowed to hold the gun, rest it on a low branch or a grass bank, and finally squeeze the trigger. And he taught me to steal any apples that might be conveniently within reach. 'Nobody,' he would say, 'ever eats all the apples off the trees. More apples go to waste than ever you saw eaten.' No doubt it was a reprehensible morality. Griff's was a world where all things were possible, and where the niceties of life seemed to matter very little. When they moved to their council house, probably because their gardener's cottage was bursting at the seams, the full complement of five children now present, I saw less of him. He seemed now to have to travel to work – probably to Butlin's Holiday Camp – and returned by bus for a rough meal before setting off around the locality to attend to various gardens. He still had time occasionally to sit in the back with his pipe, mending bikes or concocting some gadget, but less frequently. I still rode over from Madryn, along lanes whose every twist and turn I knew intimately, and there was always something happening at Glyncoed, always the rough liveliness of a house full of children. And Gwyneth was a strong, competent personality, working in the hotel when circumstances allowed, organizing her brood with a mixture of warm, defensive love, and parade-ground haranguing, and nursing Griff through attack after attack of asthma, attacks which often brought him to death's door. I never felt any sense of illness, let alone the shadow of death, in the house and never even realised the extent of the stubbornness which had dragged his unwilling body through to middle-age until the last time I saw him alive. He had acquired a patch of rough land over the road from the council estate, and I found him in it, chopping and hacking at the undergrowth, and finding, as he had done all his life, unconsidered trifles to talk about and marvel at as his sickle began to reveal the geography of his new territory. I had long since moved out from under the family umbrella into academic life, and he was engaging in his usual trenchant frivolity about earning one's living without doing any work, when he suddenly stopped hacking, sat down on a log, and fought desperately for breath for minutes on end. Then he looked up and grinned, his lips blue and his eyes deep in shadowed sockets, 'The bastard's winning,' he said. Then he got out his pipe, packed it carefully, and began to talk again about my incomprehensible life. Coming from a family which was so clearly working-class, but never knowing myself what that actually meant, it was in Griff that I found working-class attitudes richly and uncomplicatedly represented. It was in him that I caught a glimmer of the determination, the craft and the stamina that the Welsh peasant has had to develop in order to survive through all those generations of moral and physical deprivation. To survive triumphantly with wit and confidence.

Years later, when Gwyneth wrote to tell me he was dead, I remember driving up through mid-Wales with a growing sense of despair. I drove up on the day before the funeral with some intuitive sense that, infrequent though my visits had lately been, I might now be required. And so it was. I sat the night through with Gwyneth, and our talk and tea-making through the night was a fitting climax to my experience of Griff. No doubt she wept later. But that night we had no sense of grief. Only a shared joy, almost an exhilaration. He had shown us what it was to snap our fingers at circumstance. We talked the night through. I remember little of what our actual interchanges were, but I remember the openness of it all. Dawn broke, convention intervened. The spell was broken. We never met at that level again.

All around Nefyn was a magical countryside. And it was a countryside I cycled around from Dinas days on, until I came to know it yard by yard. An only child, the motivation behind my cycling expeditions was at first pure fantasy, feeding on loneliness. Philip and Roger came into my life in 1940 and left it in 1942. While they were there, life was full and real and related to the natural environment with which they gradually formed an armed neutrality, and I gradually and reluctantly learnt to share it with them. It would be wrong to suppose that either Philip or Roger ever accepted the natural world. They were moulded for ever by the city. It had made them, and they would never be able to feed on anything other than the smell and feel of it. Philip had been tamed by it, made pale and defensive behind his forelock, eyes forever slanted to meet its attack. Roger had grown strong in the speed and noise of it; small and square, he pined for it, and hated quiet places. But they both retreated into areas of themselves where they could survive, much as I myself did later when I was sent away to school. And I cluttered those areas of survival for them with endless successions of green places.

After Philip and Roger went back too soon, for whatever reason, to the city and the war, I was left to my own devices again. But I wasn't satisfied any longer to cultivate my own walled garden. I had been infected by their dissatisfaction and I needed to go further afield. The den and the field and the mill no longer fed my fantasies sufficiently, so I got on my bike and explored the world. And my bike took me to Nefyn and Griff's, and Nefyn and the fishermen, and Nefyn and exciting visitors in my grandmother's house. One route took me past Madryn Castle, and then through a tiny, deep valley called Nant Galedrydd, carpeted with flowers and shaded by very old trees. Before the road plunged into the depths of this valley, it passed a forge. And I would always stop to watch the fire burning and the bellows, and the music of the hammer on iron. I remember going there with Philip and Roger before they left, and the smith made hoops and hooks for us then and there. These, in the space of a generation, have become as obsolete as the stagecoach. But, for us, they were clearly still part of the jigsaw. One morning they became as necessary to our cycle of existence as tree-climbing was, and football, the company of mongrel dogs, and, by then, the pictures on a Saturday afternoon. It is true that, most of the time, we used car tyres, smooth as our cheeks, as substitutes; rolled them down the hill from our gate, steered them pell-mell until we had negotiated the sharp corner, and then let them jump and judder their way towards the bridge, until they eventually took a final dive into the blackthorn hedge. Traffic was no obstacle. There was no traffic. The occasional car could be heard miles away, driven at a seemly pace, giving us plenty of time to clear the decks. One day, for some reason, as often happens in childhood, the real thing became necessary. With the knowledge of absolute rejection that was so clear then, we despised car tyres as paltry, jumped on our bikes, and went to the forge at Galedrydd. I can see the sweep of tongs and hammer as the slim bar of iron, drawn sparkling out of the fire, was coaxed in one movement into a ring, and the link beaten into firm finality. The hoop was done, in a flashing moment, and the hook that was to guide it along the road came equally quickly, the final, decisive pig's-tail-curl at the end flicked onto it by the tongs. Hook and hoop were dipped in the vat of waiting cold water, and they sizzled and steamed until they were hauled out, grey and dead, and thrown onto the cobbled floor, ready for use. There weren't many horses there, but plenty of ploughshares, rakes, and bits of home-made equipment. It was a time when the farmers were becoming mechanised in a do-it-yourself style, and a time when there was no ready supply of spare parts. Everything had to be mended. And at the forge they could turn their hand to any piece of make-do-and-mend, and could indeed create a new part to replace one that had become irreparable.

⋆ ⋆ ⋆

It was from Nefyn that I discovered Nant Gwrtheyrn while I was on a solitary walk along the beach beyond Pistyll. Once again, but on foot this time, I had begun to venture beyond my normal territory. Nefyn beach might sometimes extend over the headland to the windy expanse of Morfa and on to the lifeboat station, but in the other direction it stopped where the winding hill road came past Turner's cafe and lost itself in the sand. The stonier stretches beyond, where the old wrecked pier at Pistyll was dangerous to climb on, and where the ghosts of drowned men could be heard in the wilder sea by Bird Rock, were out of my early bounds. And when I had once wandered the cliffs above with my mother to pick blackberries, a new fear was added to the others, for we saw a live viper. Vipers were not uncommon in the bracken, and there were even tales of old women dying of snake-bite. I myself had seen dead vipers before with the tell-tale jagged marks on their backs, squashed flat on roads and cart-tracks, but this one moved dry through the grass a few yards away from us, taking its poison with it. And so I dared, and walked to Pistyll Pier and beyond by myself, with the sea beating on my left, and the cliffs sheer on my right, until I began to climb on a sudden impulse, and found Nant Gwrtheyrn. Nant Gwrtheyrn in

English is Vortigen's Valley, and Vortigen was a king of the Britons whose territory lay in the region of modern Kent. His story was a desperate one, and his valley is enclosed on three sides by the great rock walls of the mountain and on the fourth side drops sheer into the sea below.

When the Romans left Britain to its own devices, every one of the Latinized British leaders, often educated in Rome, certainly imbued with Roman concepts, had a hard time of it. Harassed and invaded by the Irish, the Picts and the Scots, they found life difficult. Their patrons had departed, Roman law was a dead letter; they had to stand on their own feet. Cunedda, as we have seen, had already been sent to Gwynedd to keep order. He succeeded. Vortigen was not so lucky. The likeliest facts about what actually happened to Vortigen are contained in an amalgam of two different stories, recorded by Nennius in 796 in his *Historica Brittonum*. What seems fairly certain is that he asked the help of the Saxons of northern Europe in his efforts to subdue the Picts. And so, it is said, Hengist and Horsa and their hosts first came to the island of Britain. Vortigen had created a Frankenstein. One story says that he also, for good measure, fell in love with Hengist's daughter, and that he had to give up the Land of Kent in return for her hand. Whether that was true or not, the Saxons gradually tightened their grip, and in the end three hundred of Vortigen's trained men were slaughtered by them, and all pretence was abandoned. Vortigen himself fled westwards. His name is associated with Dinas Emrys in Snowdonia, and others speak of Caer Gwrtheyrn in Dyfed. But it is certainly just as likely – geographically more so – that he came here to Nant Gwrtheyrn to escape his pursuers who claimed that he had betrayed his people and had to die.

Let us turn to Rhabanian, the old vicar of Llandudwen, and listen to him explaining it all in his book, *Archaeologia Lleyniensis* – more a work of feverish imagination than of serious historical analysis:

> Above the unresting sea nearby, there is a fairly high hill which looks natural enough, although its summit has been somewhat flattened, and the sides marked by eight ribs from top to bottom. On this outcrop was the refuge of the supposed fugitive. Until the beginning of the last century, there was a tomb here, built of stone and covered with turf. And it was known as Vortigen's Grave . . . local tradition claims that he was buried here. Some time back, the inhabitants of the parish dug into this sacrophanus, and they found inside it a stone coffin, and within the coffin, the bones of a tall man. This discovery strengthens the tradition, as no other tomb or remains have been found in this area at all. And the fact that it had been left undisturbed for four hundred years goes a long way to suggest that someone of great dignity had been buried most carefully in such an imposing coffin, and that coffin protected in turn by such a splendid tomb.

Although the digging took place a very long time before Rhabanian came on the scene, yet these facts seem fairly firm, and the story which connects Vortigen with this place is still stubbornly alive.

Pennant did his best to keep it going:

> Fancy cannot frame a place more fit for a retreat from the knowledge of mankind, or better calculated to inspire confidence of security from pursuit.

Pennant hangs on tenaciously to the more romantic parts of Nennius's narrative, and expresses the firm belief that the story which tells of Vortigen, tracked down to this place, done to death supernaturally in a wild thunderstorm, is absolutely fitting:

> His life had been profligate; the monks therefore were determined that he should not die the common death of all men, and accordingly made him perish with signal marks of the vengeance of heaven.

The mixture of Christian love and ancient revenge begins to weave subtle confusion. Whose monks were these? What power did they serve? No doubt the legends that this place was full of ancient ghosts had led the villagers to meddle with the grave in the eighteenth century. Or perhaps they had been impelled to lay the ghosts after the most disastrous event of all had taken place.

It happened in 1750. A young man who lived in the valley, Rhys Meredydd, was to marry Meinir, also a native of the village. According to the customs of the time, the bride, on the morning of her wedding, was to run from the safety of her house, as though reluctant to marry, and hide in some not too distant spot. Her bridegroom would then have to find her personally, and carry her triumphantly to the church to be married.

The young Meinir went to hide, according to custom. She was never seen alive again. Rhys, and in time all the available villagers, hunted high and low and eventually went to the church at Clynnog in the hope that she had somehow mistakenly made her way there. But when all had gathered at Clynnog, there was no sign at all of Meinir. She had completely disappeared. So they returned silent to their homes, the harpist carrying his harp unplayed. A desolate Rhys continued to comb the woods over and over, constantly calling out Meinir's name. But there was no answer. In time, Rhys became a lonely, crazed figure, speaking to no one, his only companion his dog. His life was shattered beyond repair. And then, one day, as fairly frequently happened in such a place, a thunderstorm broke over the valley, and Rhys was out walking, oblivious of it. Then a shaft of lightning split an old treetrunk near him from top to bottom. And Meinir's corpse was revealed, trapped in what had been the rotten core of a hollow tree.

In spite of its history, and in spite of continuing legend, a quarrying community inhabited the place in modern times, and built for themselves stout houses and a school, and a chapel to worship in. But with the coming of the mobile society, it was too isolated, too difficult of access. Their derelict houses, gaping to the sky looked as benighted as any village of the damned. I knew nothing of the story when I found the place that day. It was simply an abandoned city, many of the houses still almost intact in those days, the chapel roofed and windowed, the sheep wandering in and out of doorways. There were unkempt fruit-trees tangled in gardens and there were dark, overhanging rocks above. I wandered about, buried in bracken, ensnared in briars, stared through windows, thunderstruck. What had happened? Why was it an empty world? Where were the ghosts? I didn't dare explore too much, nor stay too long, for I felt that some presence would be sure to come back, to accuse me of trespass, perhaps to trap me there for ever. I turned on my heel, and ran and slithered back down the cliff side to the sea's edge, and never asked anyone about it, never confessed that I'd found it. I dreamt about it though, and treasured it in my secret places, and always meant to return, but never did. It was years later that I first heard anyone else mention the place, and was told its stories. Then it stopped being my place and I wasn't interested in it any longer.

The medieval pilgrims would have moved past Vortigen's bolthole, oblivious to its existence, from Aelhaearn's church on the far side of Yr Eifl to Beuno's other church at Pistyll on this side. They moved through pestilence and plague, as the saints before them. The powers of darkness, in the shadow of these hills, must have seemed very close. And as they moved on through Llŷn, their path grew narrower. On either side the sea closed in.

Land is an enclosed avenue now. An arrow pointing to Bardsey. The sea licks the rocks, and all that ever happened here came from the rolling sea. The warrior saints, the solitary hermit saints, on their rock ledges, the anchorites, the healers, Beuno, Ceidio, Aelrhiw, Aelhaearn, Hywyn, Cadfan, Tudwen, almost all came by sea, looked back daily at its changing sameness and moved ever nearer their own horizon of holiness. This is the place where eternity moves in on every side; hill fort, holy well, church and solitary cell jostle for living space.

The pilgrims move on, over the shoulder of Yr Eifl, and they see before them the hills of Llŷn: Garn Boduan and the rocky outcrops around it, and then, massively, in the haze, Garn Fadryn and Garn Fach. Beyond them again, Mynydd Rhiw, Mynydd Anelog and the far breasts of Uwchmynydd. And last of all, through a central gap, the level ridge of Mynydd Enlli, Bardsey itself, swims into view.

Pistyll Church shelters below the main road, before reaching the village of Pistyll and next door to the farm, Plas Pistyll.

On the right of the path leading through the churchyard is a grave-stone with the name Thomas Michaeliones carved on it. He was the vicar of Pistyll for thirty years, but he had some diverse interests outside his work as a parish priest. He claimed to have invented the submarine, and that he had never received acknowledgement for that fact, although the patents had been properly presented. He was also the owner of one of the gold mines in Merioneth, and he would go down there to undertake some project from time to time. It could hardly be to replenish his purse.

All around the church itself in the old days was a famous herb-garden, and its plants were grown specially to treat the ills of pilgrims who came by. Some of these plants still remain, in particular about the steep banks of the stream that runs past the church door and down to the sea. The church itself is often decorated in an ancient style, with the flowers and herbs that grow around it. On the floor, clean straw is laid. As you walk in, strong herbal scents assault the nostrils. And then you notice that trees are actually growing inside the church hugging the walls.

You still feel in here a sense of sanctuary, of safety, a direct sense of shared experience with threatened early travellers: 'In here, I'm safe. Thick walls. Floor strewn with clean straw. Scent of herbs all about drives off disease. Pestilence cannot enter. Outside, plagues crowd around; the outcast and deformed peer in. The date, scrawled on the wall, 1050; Saint Christopher, my saint, saint of travellers, beside it. And signs of God abound. The cup waits on the altar. Healing water stands by the font to protect me as I leave. In here, I'm safe.'

Pilgrims were fed and watered at Pistyll as at most of the stopping places en route. Here they were fed with black bread baked by cottagers who lived nearby and who brought it to the church for that purpose. For that small service, they were excused a portion of their tithe.

* * *

Thin crust of soil, rock breaks the surface easily. Barren earth washed by the salt sea. From Pistyll back again to Nefyn along a shelf of land overhanging a spectacular sea. Thomas Pennant didn't think much of Nefyn:

> Nefyn: a miserable village, situated on an eminence at a short distance from the Western coast of Caernarfon Bay, containing (in these our modern days) no one object worthy of note . . .

And one cannot say that the old church at Nefyn is worthy of note. The 'old' church because a smart new church was built in the middle of the village many years ago now, and the old one was left to rot down among the original higgledy-piggledy streets below the hill, in real Nefyn.

But even Pennant had to admit that Nefyn had been important once. When the pilgrims arrived here, it would be a bustling point, a centre for drovers and travellers, no doubt a place where temptations would abound, the home of a thriving fishing industry. It is nevertheless perhaps with some shame that a Welshman has to confess that Pennant is right when he claims that among all this importance, Nefyn's most spectacular day was a very alien one, the celebration of Welsh defeat:

> . . . in former times it was honoured with a royal visit and a magnificent tournament. Here Edward I held his triumph on the conquest of Wales, and to conciliate his new subjects, in imitation of their hero, Arthur, held a round table, and celebrated it with a dance and tournament. The concourse was

> prodigious; for not only the chief nobility of England, but numbers from foreign parts, graced the festival with their presence. Marks of honour were distributed on this occasion with a bounty truly royal . . .

Marks of honour were no doubt necessary, as a compensation for those Norman lords who had travelled weary distances for an entirely worldly reason on materialistic pilgrimage. They must have poured imprecations on the head of a king who chose to have such a concourse in such a place.

But Nefyn remained both important and Welsh. In later centuries, it continued to be the centre of Llŷn's fisheries, and to be a ship-building centre too:

> 1748; a sea wall was this year built at Nefyn which will be of great benefit to the fishermen of the locality. During the last twelve months 5,000 barrels of salt fish were exported from this port to Ireland and elsewhere, not to mention those which were eaten in England . . .

And in any case, Nefyn is my place. I was born here. I spent my summers here long after we moved away. I knew it inch by inch. I knew nothing of tournaments and Norman splendour. But I heard of sloops and schooners, and listened to old men on the clifftop who remembered the bay boiling with ships and dragnets as far as the eye could see. I was born here, and I knew there was nothing in life more important than the sea.

Nor in death either. The most telling thing

about the old church in Nefyn by now is the graveyard. Stone after stone tells stories of that other pilgrimage that Llŷn has always known. Even in my generation, two of my cousins went to sea, and the wanderlust is such, the lack of parochialism in this place is such, that one of them lives in Canada, another in South Africa, and a third maintains oil-rigs in the North Sea. Sloops and schooners, built in Nefyn, sailed the world. And many died in the process:

> Richard Parry, Master of the brig, 'Endeavour' of this port, who fell off the Board near Yr Eifl, and drowned on the 25th September, 1831, aged 24 years . . .

A Master at 24, he must have looked forward to many transatlantic voyages, perhaps to glory at sea. But the sea claimed him as finally as if he'd died rounding Cape Horn in a south-westerly gale, as others buried in this graveyard did. Drunken gravestones, leering out of the long grass and the brambles, speak of the sea.

During the last century, there was much talk of Porthdinllaen, Nefyn's neighbouring bay, becoming the embarkation point for the packet boat to Ireland. There was great excitement:

> If the new projected road to Ireland through this part of Wales succeeds, and packet-boats are established at the fine and commodious harbour of Porth-ddyn-lleyn, Nefyn may again see better days, and once more flourish in trade and opulence . . .

It never happened. After bitter dispute, the Irish trade went to Holyhead, to what was clearly an inferior harbour. And in Porthdinllaen those rusty iron rings that once tethered schooners beneath the cliffs of home when they returned from Rio, and brought parrots and monkeys with them to prove it, remained there for us in my childhood to tether our dreams to.

Summer by summer I would weave my way through Nefyn and Morfa Nefyn, through rows of tourist bungalows, to the open bay at Porthdinllaen. It has been all of a piece, the coming and going in these villages. The saints came from the sea and perched on its shore. The medieval pilgrims knew it hemmed them in on both sides. And those who have lived here ever since have always looked outwards. From the depth of their roots in a past impregnated with a sense of the eternal, they have themselves been explorers, searching for something unknown, their eyes constantly on distant horizons.

Recently, walking those paths again, I had two memories as I sat and watched the sea. Memories of two men. I remembered fishing for rock salmon off the rocks with Griff. We would walk over the golf links, the wind in our faces, past the place where the sea had worn a tunnel through the rocks up to a funnelling hole in the green turf. You could stand by the rickety fence, half-heartedly erected around the hole after an old man, trying to find his way home one Saturday night, tumbled down it to his death, and hear the roar of the sea echoing in the tunnel. Then we would sit on the rocks and hope for rock salmon. We never caught any. Griff was no fisherman. Not for him the long wait for fish. He preferred the activity of stalking rabbits. But we sat and stared at the sea, on perilous edges where the water sucked and licked around us, got gradually, proudly, soaked, and went home happy. And I remember being on the outermost point with my father – the wind tearing at us as always, and watching a sailing-boat tacking into the lee-side of Porthdinllaen, surging in through the white breakers, swivelling into shelter and smoothly coming to rest far down below. My father sighed and turned away. Some longing for a life he had lost sight of constantly drove him to cliffside walks, to long, solitary sessions by the sea, often in the wind and rain. The fact that I was with him that day was a fact he hardly noticed.

# V

I had already gone away to school when we moved to Gelliwig. I went away to school at eleven, partly, I think, because my father was clearly eager to ensure success for me in the great world, and partly, no doubt, as a result of patronage from Nanhoron. As with many others, so with me, leaving Llŷn to attend a prep school in Shrewsbury only deepened my attachment for my own locality. I always dreaded the process of separation. The pull of the locomotive as it tugged the train out of Pwllheli remains a sentient experience even now. I would sit miserably in my corner and watch the harbour slowly slide away, and then stare at the strange landscape beyond Pwllheli, until the tears finally came and everything merged for a while into an indeterminate mist. Leaving Llŷn, from the first step out of our house early on the dreaded morning in my school clothes, caused me physical pain. I would feel, as I awoke, a dull ache in my stomach, and a heaviness hung over the whole landscape. I said goodbye to everything as though for the last time, quietly and privately. I looked up at the permanent bulk of Y Garn and envied it. And I treasured every sight of every bend in the road until we finally turned into the station yard at Pwllheli. And in a sense it was true that I was saying goodbye for the last time. For every return was an awkward new beginning. School terms from now on split my life in half and taught me, rapidly and effectively, the art of acting. At home, I lived. In school, I acted. And I survived. But the story of that survival does not belong to this narrative. It had nothing to do with Llŷn. From the moment I left Pwllheli station on that first morning, I lived in two worlds, unrelated and quite deliberately kept in different compartments of my heart and mind. The world of school was the world where I learnt to hide feelings, to develop a convenient social hypocrisy, to look after number-one, to compete, to pretend to be English; the world of Llŷn was the place where none of this was called for; there I could go back to being myself again.

And so, if the process of leaving Pwllheli station, when I was seventeen just as much as during that first traumatic year when I was just eleven, was an unmixed misery, the process of returning to it was ecstasy. I can recall the joyous excitement of standing on the station at Afon Wen in the December dusk at the beginning of the Christmas holidays. Afon Wen was the junction, three miles from Pwllheli, where the old London, Midland and Scottish line from Caernarfon through Eifionydd met the Great Western's Cambrian Coast line from Barmouth and Porthmadog. When I was at Shrewsbury, I would come via the Cambrian Coast, but when I moved on to

Denstone, my public school in Staffordshire, at fourteen, I came by way of Bangor and Caernarfon. Both routes would take me through country that was mystically Welsh. The Cambrian Coast line hit the grey sea at Aberdyfi and hugged the coast all the way. I would normally be travelling that way in the late afternoon, and the declining sun sparkled across the sea, and the sky reddened as the sun declined. And across the sea too, visible on all but the saddest winter days, was the humped serpent of Llŷn. I could see Y Garn, and then Mynydd Rhiw, and then Uwchmynydd, and finally, across a gap, Bardsey Island. The LMS meandered across Eifionydd, surely one of the most leisurely schedules even that easy-going line ever devised. We would stop at flowery gravel platforms for long minutes, and people would chat, and the porter would investigate the nature of the train's cargo, and eventually we would move on. Penygroes, Bryncir, Pant Glas, Chwilog. At Pant Glas, my father long since had manned the signal-box at night, taking his theology books with him and his flask and sandwiches. And cronies used to call, challenge his aspirations to scholarship. And he would lead them on, talk the hind legs off them. And the night would slip by. It was in Pant Glas that he met my mother. He would pass the smithy on his way to the signal-box, arriving late, no doubt, for the night shift.

So I would arrive, by one route or the other, at Afon Wen. Whichever route I came by, the train never seemed to be a through train to Pwllheli. Many people cursed Afon Wen bitterly in my hearing. A long, draughty platform, in the middle of nowhere, and often an hour or more to wait for the only connection. You could almost have saved time by walking to Pwllheli. But for me, especially in winter, it was full of excitement. I could afford to wait and savour in my imagination all the freedoms in store. So I deliberately walked up the wooden steps of the footbridge that crossed the line, and stood there, in the teeth of the wind from the sea. I let it batter my coat against me, hurl my hair against the sky, and the escape from regimentation was all I desired – to be alive and to be back.

Some years ago, they demolished it. My mother told me that they simply dug a huge hole, and shovelled the station into it, lock, stock, and barrel. No one, of course, thought this remarkable. We shall leave few monuments. We prefer to obliterate them. But the ghosts of thousands of commuting Methodist ministers, eisteddfod adjudicators, sailors and emigrants to Liverpool, must haunt that marshland grave.

I must have been drawing near the end of my time at my prep school when we moved to Gelliwig. I'm still not certain why we moved. Something to do, no doubt, with changing times. The house at Madryn was probably very saleable. Gelliwig clearly wasn't. But moving there was like crossing an ocean and arriving in a different world. Gelliwig was an old, secluded Tudor-built manor-house, attached to the Nanhoron estate as a dower-house in Botwnnog, but dilapidated and neglected by the time we arrived there. Plas

Nanhoron stands some two or three miles to the north, and was the home of an important local family of Welsh gentry for generations. The family was originally called Edwards, and later Lloyd-Edwards, and they were prominent in the public life of the county of Caernarfon during the time of Cromwell. Richard Edwards of Nanhoron was an early and committed Puritan, and became a member of the Caernarfonshire Committee when the system of county committees became an integral part of the Puritan administrative structure. He, along with four other gentry of Llŷn, was imprisoned in Caernarfon gaol, soon after the Restoration, as a potential trouble-maker, and a cache of arms was later found in Nanhoron. Richard Edwards was clearly a man of principle, and the records show him as a counsellor, the soundness of whose advice was highly valued, and he was later released and even took part in public life once again. After his death in 1704, the family produced soldiers, sailors and clergy, but, in the main, sailors, and the most prominent perhaps was Captain Timothy Edwards, who fought with distinction in the West Indies in the 1770s, and was famous as one of the leading captains of Ships of the Line of that period. His wife, Catherine, went on the long coach journey to Portsmouth to greet his return from a successful campaign in July, 1780, only to discover, when the ship landed, that he had died of yellow fever, and been buried at sea. Catherine Edwards, alone and destitute in Portsmouth, was then, it is said, so well-treated and cared for by members of puritan sects there that she determined to join their faith, and re-established the link between Nanhoron and puritan non-conformists when, on her return home, she became a member of the congregation in one of the first non-conformist chapels in Wales, Capel Newydd, which still stands, preserved on the Nanhoron estate, a mile or so from the house itself. Gelliwig was originally built by a less notable local dignitary for his own use, but was acquired by the Nanhoron estate from a family of Joneses in the eighteenth century, and thereafter used as a dower house. Early in the twentieth century, the daughter of Nanhoron, Mary, married an army officer of Anglo-Irish extraction, Alan Gough, and took up residence in Gelliwig, while her brother ran the estate from Nanhoron. Alan Gough died young, and when her brother died also, Mary Gough moved to Nanhoron to become in due time an old lady whom I visited on Sunday afternoons. Gelliwig in turn was left to muse on past splendours.

We were certainly ill-equipped to restore them. We arrived there early one autumn evening, our furniture transported in a lorry hired from a friend in the parish, and proceeded to add our meagre contribution to the collection of dignified, in some cases elegant and distinguished, furniture that already decorated the house. One approaches it from Botwnnog, turning off the main road where the large, Victorian chapel, Rhydbach, stands at the entrance to the village. The side road then wanders along for a mile or so, passing on the right another side road that will eventually lead to the villages of Bryncroes and Rhiw, and finally entering the covert of trees that completely hides the house from public view.

As one rounds the final bend in the drive, shadowed as it was then, and indeed still is, by overhanging branches, and grass-grown in the middle, Gelliwig itself comes quietly into view. Quietly, for it is itself overhung by trees, partly ivy-covered, and a great, spreading magnolia climbs up the wall around the front door. It is long and low, and beautifully and calmly proportioned. Even in its decrepitude, a place of grace and dignity. I know that I felt its atmosphere at once. And I feel it still. That first evening, we lugged and hauled chairs and boxes and sofas until the dusk had deepened into darkness, and then we sat in the big kitchen, painted with soft shadows by the yellow light of our Aladdin lamp, and ate corned beef and chutney. Along the kitchen wall was a row of bells, sprung and numbered, and after gulping my meal, I rushed around the house ringing them from room to room. The foyer was modest, but a finer balanced staircase curved upwards out of it, and opposite the front door was a drawing-room the like of which I had never seen before. In it was a grand piano, a spinning-wheel, a broken harp, many pictures, a fireplace at each end, silver ornaments, things of stately and unimaginable richness. A row of long windows looked out through half-closed shutters, on the darkness outside. The dining room was smaller, but equally strange and darkly panelled. Members of the Nanhoron family looked down from its walls, and the shining table filled the room with massive solidity. Upstairs, an arched corridor contained collections of coral, books, moths, butterflies. First of all, awkwardly, by the light of my torch, I saw row after row of books bound in illuminated leather, arranged from floor to ceiling in glass-fronted bookshelves. Further along were the display-cases where narrow slivers of drawers opened out to show the fastidiously labelled collections. The main bedrooms had dressing-rooms opening off them, and even the lavatories seemed built for a different species, with steps leading up to the actual toilet itself. And then, opening off the central area, were dark, narrow rabbit-warrens where the domestic army no doubt silently retired. Those were empty, desolate boxes, sad and ghost-ridden, and I retreated rapidly from them. But when I eventually went to my own room at the top of that sweeping staircase, carrying my candle past a tattered regimental-standard and the crossed spears and taut brown shield that were the grim prizes of some African expedition, it was certainly hours before I slept. It is difficult to estimate the immediate impact of such a confrontation on the mind of a sheltered thirteen year old. Suddenly I had been catapulted into an alien, but a fiercely exciting, environment. It was an environment where you were surrounded, not only by the necessities of life, but by an endless array of beautiful things, pictures, musical instruments, glittering furniture. Even the wallpaper seemed to belong to a different order of existence. I know that Gelliwig in no way impressed me as an isolated and deserted place. It seemed that night to be frighteningly alive. As I lay in bed, and heard the chorus of ravens consulting in the trees, a stream of images, sharp and insistent, passed through my mind. Images from the fiction that I had already read, images of cavaliers and highwaymen, lairds and lords and chieftains, Bonnie Prince Charlie and the Scarlet Pimpernel, Llywelyn and Captain Morgan and Nelson, all suddenly endowed with new reality. Weary of excitement, a child once more, let loose in a secret garden, I fell asleep.

And when morning came, I continued to wander thunderstruck around this new treasure-house. I looked more carefully at the faces of the men and women on the wall, at the startlingly similar rosy-cheeked women, and at the arrogant men under three-cornered hats. Chins thrust out, eyes impudent, hand on sword, they were all warriors. And then I ventured out of doors. It was easy to imagine the overgrown lawns sweetly cut and the flower-beds red with roses, and the small, ornamental lake, now muddy and dark, reflecting the willows and pampas grass growing around it. I found it very easy to imagine it peopled by those men and women, and I could see them walking all around me, arm in arm through the arched and walled gardens, playing croquet on the green terrace. And I, wandering alone past the peach-tree in the ruins of the walled garden, picking my way through the litter of Victoria Plums, rotting away on the path, came across a dog's cemetery in the overgrown orchard. With proper gravestones, and dates of birth and death, and English names, Rover and Boy. I experienced Gelliwig then, inside and out, as a supernova in the limited universe of my life. It exploded before my consciousness and changed the nature of the world.

Our own life at Gelliwig was frugal, isolated, simple and solitary, our diet sometimes supplemented by the pheasant my father would bring home from Nanhoron, and constantly augmented by cartloads of swedes, rabbits, butter, cabbages and buttermilk from every farm in the parish. But it also happened that my sudden insight into the different dimensions life might contain was reinforced by my own contacts with the gentry.

When I came home on holiday, a Sunday arrangement was arrived at which ensured this. My father was now, of course, inconveniently situated as far as his churches were concerned. He was in fact living in another parson's parish. So, on Sundays, he and my mother would set off in the morning for their row of services in the two churches, they would eat a picnic lunch in the church at Llaniestyn, and continue with Sunday School there, coming home for a tea-break before their final evening service. I would very occasionally accompany them on this circuit, but I would frequently be invited instead to make my way to Nanhoron for lunch, and be picked up by my parents on their way home for tea. I would even, on rare occasions, stay there for tea as well.

Mrs Gough was by now blind and crippled with arthritis, so she was totally confined to her room. I would therefore eat lunch with her official Lady's

Companion, one of a number that I met. Occasionally there would be a house-guest, but those were few and far between. Most of the time I was talked to by the Companion. There was still a butler at Nanhoron, and I grew accustomed to walking up to the front door, pulling at the brass bell-pull, and being admitted as Master Jones. I would then be ushered into the library, and given *The Times* and the Sunday papers to read. We never took Sunday papers – although Griff, of course, did – and I was certainly unfamiliar with the dark columns of *The Times*. I came to know that I would be left there for an hour or so before anything else happened, so, having prowled around the shelves and made a thorough examination of whatever else had been left lying about, I would tackle the sports pages of *The Times*, and the advertisement columns, reading half-understood accounts of polo and real tennis and rugby fives, and glorying in the messages in the personal columns that I knew had been food and drink to Sherlock Holmes. Then the gong would sound, and I would be led into the dining-room. Every time, even though the Companion and I would be the only ones to occupy the great table, all the formal etiquette of gracious living was duly observed As a matter of fact, I enjoyed those lunches hugely, strangely cooked vegetables served in silver dishes, and spices and sauces that I had never encountered before; and cider. Always cider in a small silver tankard. Then I would retreat again to the library, where coffee would be brought. If the butler brought the coffee, the air of ludicrous dignity would be maintained. But sometimes the cook would bring it, or a girl from the kitchen, and they were not prepared to play the game. They talked to me in Welsh, and pulled my leg, and walked away laughing. And it was, of course, a game. I wore the persona of the little master with inward glee, and learnt to respond to the dry questioning of the butler with equally laconic answers.

Sometimes, I would be called to the presence of Mrs Gough herself. The Companion would lead me up to a tiny morning-room leading out of her bedroom from where, had she been sighted, she could have looked out at her green parkland and the man-made pattern of her trees. A bony hand held a silver-topped stick, and her legs were covered by a huge shawl. She seemed very old, shrivelled and gaunt. But I was neither afraid of her nor repelled by her. Although her precise, cultured English was strange, and did indeed belong to another age, our relationship was not unpleasant. She assumed I was a human being. She addressed me as an equal. And she asked sharp and pointed questions, never wasting time on the kind of awkward patronising one usually had to endure from adults. She asked me about school, perfunctorily, but she asked much more pressingly about the locality. And I soon found that that was where my research had to be thorough. I had to find out who was ill, and who was getting married. Nevertheless, she often made what I looked upon as unjustifiable assumptions regarding my omniscience, and was disappointed when I failed to come up to the mark. Were there sheep in such and such a field? What was the state of the beech trees along the drive? Had such and such a farm been sold? I can only suppose that I was being used to check on the accuracy of the reports she was receiving from her various employees. On summer afternoons, instead of going into the library, I would be served coffee on the veranda, and there, static for two-and-a-half hours before my parents arrived, I would sit and read. In the Nanhoron library I discovered Thomas Hardy, and the English poets, especially Tennyson, heavily bound. I was not a studious boy. My achievements in school, such as they were, were sporting. I was a Philistine. It was only here, on these afternoons, that I began to read for pleasure. I read long swathes of 'Tess', long before I understood any of its implications, and I looked up from its pages, and saw the breeze playing through the far trees, and felt some intimation of things I knew nothing about.

Around my base in Gelliwig, although I knew nothing consciously of that either, the whole countryside was redolent with legends, with ancient history, and with shades of the supernatural. Myrddin recounts a tale of the farm 'Trewen', and says, quite seriously, that the 'little people' were in the habit of visiting the farmer. They would come to wash in a nearby stream, and sometimes they would cross it in boats made of the bark of willow and mountain-ash. Then they would visit the house to pay compensation for the damage caused to the pasture as they tramped around in great numbers. They would always leave a piece of silver beneath a milking pail, and the result was that the family who lived there became very rich. Somehow, however, the farmer offended the little people, they withdrew their favours, and his fortunes immediately changed, until he finally became destitute and had to sell the farm. And many of the farms in this immediate locality are very old, whether legends attach to them or not. They shelter behind grey walls, and are often effectively hidden away from the public gaze by those walls, by the high blackthorn hedges, and by the twists and turns of the lanes that lead to them. Neigwl Plas, on the way to the sea, at the foot of Mynydd Rhiw, owes its name to the Norman, Nigel de Lohareyn, who received the charters of Pwllheli and Nefyn, and an old Welsh ballad describes a terrible fire that once burnt the whole place down and killed the family in their beds. Nearby too are Saethon and Rhydolion, the homes of gentry whose history goes back to the Welsh princes. Siaffre Parry of Rhydolion was one of Cromwell's preaching ministers, and recruited people for the Puritan cause by praying for them in public.

Here too are many wells to which stories are attached. Ffynnon Saethon, carved out of the rock near Saethon itself, attracted pilgrims, and it was said that girls who were eager to know whether their sweethearts loved them truly should throw a pin into the well. If the pin floated, all was well; if not, it was time she looked elsewhere. And Ffynnon Sarff, nearer Nanhoron, had a different kind of distinction. As its name implies there was a strong belief that a serpent lived in it. Myrddin suggests that the most credible version of the story is that a nest of poisonous snakes lived near the well, and came to it regularly to drink. In such a locality, ghost stories were ten-a-penny, but a stubborn and well-documented one attached itself to Gelliwig. A noisy and ill-disposed ghost apparently caused great concern and discomfort to the Joneses of Gelliwig at one time. So they sought a well-known exorcist, a Mr Williams, who was the Rector of Llanengan. A terrible struggle then ensued between the ghost and the exorcist, and the Rector emerged from the locked room where the struggle had taken place utterly exhausted, his coat and trousers torn and a dreadful stench emanating from his clothing. The exorcism, however, seems to have been successful. Peace returned to the house.

One could go on. It is the sort of locality where legends attach to houses, wells, crossroads, groves of trees. Everywhere is touched by the light of intense experience. It is the sort of place of which Myrddin himself writes:

> Some ghost lives at the foot of every hedge, a dead man's candle lights every church, a white lady watches over every crossroads, and spectres are as frequent as gorse bushes . . .

As for me, my bike cotinued to take me all over Llŷn. And now my routes to Nefyn and elsewhere were complicated by the pangs of first love. There were two girls, at different times, about whom I found it necessary to weave amorous fantasies. I rode unnecessarily past their homes, taking laborious long-cuts in order to do so, in the often vain hope of catching a glimpse of whichever was commanding my imagination at the time. If I did see the one who mattered, and stopped and talked, I would go over and over the words we had used as I rode home, the number of times she had smiled, how she looked as she moved in a summer dress, how slim girls' waists were, how their eyes moved around, sometimes searching out some hidden meaning, sometimes dismissive and contemptuous. You never knew where you were with them, you couldn't talk to them naturally as you could with boys. But then you didn't want to. You wanted them to be different and mysterious, to smell strangely and to turn away as they smiled. This was what girls were for. One of my torturers lived on a farm on the slopes of Garn Fadryn, and the other, before her family moved away, some distance out of the village of Llaniestyn. Neither of these lingering affairs came to much. I got as far as exchanging passionate letters with one of them after some shy and inconclusive encounters in dark lanes. I had become acceptable to her family and went there for tea. And then we walked the fields of her farm above Nanhoron Valley, gathered nuts in autumn, scuffed our feet through the mown hay and finally sat, once only, high up in the traditional haystack and, holding hands, had our first French kiss. My parents discovered our passionate correspondence and were outraged. She was not suitable. It was not to continue. I was shattered and disillusioned. I surrendered and obeyed, but life was never so perfect again. I would remember for a long time the way her hair bounced on her shoulders as she walked out of church, her blue print dress rounded by her thighs when she sat on the hillside, plucking dead dandelions and blowing them into the wind. And her secret smile looked out at me from a forbidden photograph for years after she had gone off unashamed to have a baby by a mechanic from Sarn. I remember the first time I saw her in church, sitting with him, staring down at her feet. He was a small man, years older than we were, wrinkles on his face, oil beneath his fingernails. Why had she chosen him? How did these things happen? She didn't speak to any of us as we hung around the church gate that Sunday. She just went with him, got into his van and drove away. How did these things happen? We didn't know. We knew very little. The other girl remained my untouchable Beatrice, beautiful and distant, until a brief recriminatory foray during university days finally put paid to that image as well. She was as mortal as the rest and so, by that time, was I.

As with all romantic dreams, however, the existence of my first loves, unobtainable and only vaguely desired, coloured the landscape and added another dimension to those roads and lanes that led past their homes. My lack of realistic achievement with these girls might eventually have been depressing if I had been at home all the time, but, as it was, it was all of a piece with the quality of a world that was so much in the mind. There were other, more attainable targets, stolen escapades from my boarding school, town girls who pressed their bodies against you and laughed, girls you met in chip-shops and took into dark streets. But they were not romantic and they belonged to another world. They have no part in this account, as the others have. They brought me a sort of knowledge that was alien then and remained so for a long time. The real animal joy of life at home when I was growing up was not sex but rudimentary football. At school, I played rugby and cricket, like any other English public-schoolboy. Soccer was frowned on. At home, everyone played soccer all the year round, but especially in the summer. There was a field below the church in Llaniestyn where we played, and then, on summer evenings, we would travel on bikes and motor-bikes to places like Edern and Mynytho to play challenge matches against their teams. I would subsequently arrive home at all hours, bearing in mind that I might well be taking a hopeful roundabout route, and on one occasion the whole thing led to disaster. I had been playing in Llaniestyn on a summer evening, and set off to ride home, sweaty and dirty, still wearing my football boots. When I got to Botwnnog, after passing the church and school, there was a steep hill leading down to the Pwllheli–Aberdaron road. The orthodox route was to turn left in the direction of Rhydbach chapel, and then right along a country lane. But immediately opposite my entry into the main road was a bumpy path that provided a convenient short-cut. It wasn't therefore unusual for me to hurtle down the hill, straight across the main road, and down the path for home. I still maintain that on this occasion I was more careful than usual. But not careful enough. I could swear that I stopped by the Post Office, and that I then started off across the road. When I was half way across and glanced to my right, time stood still. A car was bearing down on me. I remember remaining quite calm, and making a conscious decision that the only possible course of action was to tread hard on the pedals and reach the other side before it hit me. I attempted it. And I failed. The car caught the back wheel of the bike, made mincemeat of it, went out of control and ran into the hedge. I was thrown face-first onto the road, but fortunately clear of the flailing car and bike. It didn't hurt, I remember. I was simply flying through the air, and then suddenly brought up short. All was still quite clear and unhurried. I got up, felt a pulpy mess somewhere around my right eye, saw my hand covered with blood, and then noticed that there seemed to be a group of spectators lined up in front of the Post Office.

'I think I ought to see a doctor,' I said, in Welsh. There was no discernible response, as far as I can remember. And then a car drew up, a man leapt out, bundled me in, and drove me off to the doctor's house around the corner. On the way, I caught a glimpse of the car in the hedge and its occupants still sitting in it. I was taken into a front room of the imposing doctor's house, Llys Meddyg, that stares across from a superior height at Rhydbach chapel. A doctor was summoned from somewhere, and performed on what turned out to be a long, deep and jagged cut a fraction of an inch above my right eye. My parents were very calm. I was put to bed. My face, when I was allowed to see it next day, was a patchwork of cuts and abrasions, but nothing was actually broken. Later, a police constable came and asked questions nicely about the whole thing, and I chatted amicably with him. Later still, he turned up again with a summons to appear in Pwllheli Magistrates Court to answer a charge of Dangerous Riding of a Pedal Cycle. That seemed to me to be adding insult to injury, and my father, who ultimately paid the fine, vociferously agreed. There was a lawless streak in both of us, and this certainly served to deepen it. All officials of the state, all uniformed executants of secular authority, from clerks to Chief Superintendents, my father regarded with distaste and distrust, and he was always ready to engage them in conflict. He would certainly go out of his way to help the most palpable rogue against them. It was simply another aspect of his many-sided independence of mind that this attitude, carrying with it, as it did, an unwillingness to accept at face value any authority of any kind, still had no difficulty in co-existing with a continuing high regard for all things military. The military were the only people who wore proper uniforms and deserved to wear them. I believe this attitude was deepened by a disturbing element in his life while he was at Birkenhead. Part of his duties there had involved acting as part-time chaplain to

Welsh-speaking prisoners in Walton Gaol. It affected him deeply. Doggedly rebellious as he already was, the clank of keys, the shutting out of the sun, moved him to anger. And he was moved too by the obvious inadequacy of those he was trying to minister to. He found, he would say, little evil in there, only incompetence. It all came to a head when it was going to be part of his job to be present at an execution and read the prayers. He saw that it was impossible, gave up his job, and never, to my knowledge, had anything to do with the forces of law and order again.

The incident with the bike was, in a way, the end of my life in Llŷn. The bike was totally wrecked. I was, after all, about to go to university in Bangor, having made a conscious decision that I must return from my foreign schools to Wales. And suddenly, during the weeks I spent out of circulation, waiting for my face to mend, I wrote a novel. Feverishly, in a private book, day after day of that warm summer. Written, of course, in English, the language of my education. A long novel about growing up and being Welsh and about roots. I destroyed it soon after. And I don't remember what I said in it. And I certainly didn't confess to my friends that I had started writing novels. But I could see that life was changing. And my desire, even then, to record what was past, arose from a feeling that things might not be changing for the better.

# VI

Aberdaron and Bardsey Island only became an integral part of my jigsaw of Llŷn after I had left. But they are now so important, if only as symbols of the way of life I knew in Nefyn and Dinas and Llaniestyn and Gelliwig, that they must be included. Everything in Aberdaron smacks of Bardsey. You can see three roads leading into the village, one from Rhoshirwaun and Sarn Mellteyrn, one from Rhiw and Hell's Mouth, and the third from Uwchmynydd. And from each direction, the roads descend steep hills before meeting at the bridge that crosses two rivers at the focal point of the village.

The beach is open, and the breakers beat against it most days. From the eastern end, Trwyn y Penrhyn, to the westerly headland where the River Saint meanders into the sea through a narrow gulley, the sand is grey and stony, and the sea is often rough enough to leave a substantial tidemark of seaweed and flotsam. The swell has always been so threatening here that it was never the normal practice to use Aberdaron as the embarkation point for Bardsey. It was from Porth Meudwy, beyond the westerly headland, from a small, much less exposed inlet, that the monks used to set off for the priory on the island, and it's from Porth Meudwy that the few remaining travellers journey to Bardsey today.

I have already started talking about Bardsey. But Aberdaron does have its own identity. Saint Hywyn's church is now on the seashore. Considerable erosion has eaten away at the shoreline over the centuries, so much so that the church was once thought to be in a perilous position, and in danger of being undermined completely. One blind, windowless wall faces the sea, and this is a testimony not so much to the extreme age of the church as to the wildness of the winter sea on a stormy night. It also bears witness to the fact that Aberdaron not only looks out towards Bardsey, but also towards an open and treacherous sea. I have been in the church at Aberdaron as a boy when October gales were howling outside, and the threatening, flickering shadows inside the building only lent further credence to the compelling fantasy that one was aboard ship crossing a dark ocean.

If you round the easterly point of the bay and cut across the small inlets of Porth Cadfan and Porth Ysgo, you will come to the jaws of Hell's Mouth, one of the most unprotected lengths of open beach in Britain. Ships have been wrecked on the rocks at either end, especially on Trwyn Cilan, which stands between it and the comparative calm of Porth Ceiriad and Abersoch. Hell's Mouth and Aberdaron both face the prevailing south-westerlies, which often sweep hard across them.

In Abersoch Bay, there are two islands named

after Saint Tudwal, and on the larger of the two there used to be a chapel, and a cell, the remains of yet another hermit's resting-place. This particular island is sheltered enough to breed sheep on, but every one who writes about these parts stresses the dangers from the sea. Samuel Lewis, in his topographical dictionary published in 1833, emphasises it, and Pennant too refers often to Sarn Badrig, the sandbank that runs right along the whole length of Llŷn on the south side and ends opposite Aberdaron.

If we return along the road that led us to Hell's Mouth, we can get a glimpse of the importance of this locality in ancient times. From the top of the steep hill that leads to the village of Rhiw, looking back to Hell's Mouth, Myrddin tells us that we can actually see no fewer than five holy wells, and some of them notable ones. He writes, for example, about Ffynnon Aelrhiw, near the church at Rhiw:

> Many sick pilgrims travelled to it to obtain Saint Aelrhiw's blessing, and to sample its virtues . . .

He writes more specifically about Ffynnon Cefn Lleithfan, on the eastern side of the mountain, in the parish of Bryncroes:

> Its shape is angular, about two yards wide and strongly walled around. Steps lead down into it from two directions. Many come to it from near and far, especially those who were troubled by external cancers, for which its water was considered of great goodness . . .

This reference is interesting, for another term for an external cancer in Gwynedd Welsh is 'dafad wyllt', a wild, or malignant wart. Until very recently, the 'dafad wyllt man' lived near Aberdaron. Owen Griffith, Penycaerau, was an amateur without any kind of medical qualification, but there's no doubt that he and his family before him had an entirely effective treatment for a complaint that could be more than troublesome. Indeed, so my father said anyhow, it could prove fatal if it was not properly treated. Those dealing with animals seemed quite frequently to be affected in this way, and I remember going in the car with my father to take someone or other to Penycaerau. The man had a bandage about his head, and the strict instruction was that the sufferer was not to touch the cancer at all or meddle with it in any way, and he was certainly not to visit a conventional doctor with it. He was to rely totally on Owen Griffith's treatment. The cancer would then work its way out without fail, with its root attached to it, leaving the face – and it was on the face that it usually appeared – unscarred. As far as I know, this remarkable ability to deal with something that orthodox medical practice then found basically incurable has never been adequately passed on to anyone else.

Apart from the evidence of the wells, there are other signs of very ancient activity in the locality of Rhiw, activity that goes back to neolithic times. On the south-westerly fringes of the mountain, near Hell's Mouth, there are two important ancient monuments, one of them only recently discovered. One is an old burial-chamber near the manor-house of Plas-yn-Rhiw, and the other is one of the few Stone Age axe factories that have so far been discovered. Along this road too above Porth Ysgo, on a spectacular site, the old church of Llanfaelrhys rises out of the rock. It must have been a comforting sight to many a sailor returning home around the far headland.

This, it seems, was the place where Maelrhys ab Gwyddno ab Emyr Llydaw established his cell. Maelrhys came here with Cadfan and Bywyn, and he too went to Bardsey in his turn. He must have been satisfied that he had placed himself entirely in the hands of providence as the dark winter closed around him here and the storms began to drive against the dry stone walls of his cell.

There's another story about the establishing of Llanfaelrhys which is repeated both by Rhabanian and Myrddin, as well as by many others, although Myrddin, as he tells the story, also castigates those who go around repeating such obviously fantastic tales:

> Once, when these parts had sunk into grave hunger through lack of food, a man called Rhys landed here from Southern parts with a ship's cargo of flour, and set himself up as a supplier of flour to the inhabitants. He profited greatly from this enterprise (the Welsh word Myrddin uses for profit is 'maeliodd') and as he saw that the locality had no place set aside for the worship of God, he voluntarily gave his profits for the building of a small church, and that is how the name Llanfaelrhys (the Llan of Rhys's profit) came to be . . .

Far from the historical facts certainly. But it tells us something of subsistence-living in a place like this, and the need for kindly legends to raise men's hopes and spirits. And, as a matter of fact, there is a farmhouse called Blawtty (Flour-store) in the neighbourhood!

If we return to Aberdaron, we will see on our right another farmhouse of some importance. Bodwrdda is, in fact, more of a manor-house than a farm and stands in its grove of trees on the river bank to the right of the road. The flour-mill and fulling-mill – for treating sheep's wool – that were almost always part of the compound of a manor-house in Wales in the Middle Ages, still stand, and a glance at what remains of the old complex of buildings shows the extent to which the family seat would be a self-sufficient unit in every way possible. This was, of course, particularly necessary in a place as isolated as this.

Looking at the family of Wynns or Gwynnes who used to live here, one is struck yet again by the cosmopolitan confidence and high achievement of some of these Llŷn families. There was nothing passively parochial about them. Rooted in a remarkable countryside, and always returning to it as to a mother's care, they nevertheless moved confidently and even arrogantly into the great world. It was the Parrys of Madryn who financed much of the Patagonian expedition of 1865. The Wynnes of Cefnamlwch were outstanding in the public life of North Wales and one of them became Bishop of Bangor in 1633 (in fact, at least six Bishops of Bangor were born within a ten mile radius of Garn Fadryn). The Edwards family of Nanhoron sent out numerous soldiers and sailors, including an outstanding sea-captain in Timothy Edwards, and the Wynns, too, made their mark. Owen Gwyn became Principal of St John's College, Cambridge, in the sixteenth century, and a later Gwynn, Griffith Gwynn, who was born in 1621, was one of the delegation who went to Paris to bring the restored King Charles II back to London.

If we return to Aberdaron, and then make our way along the second road that leads in and out of the village, the road to Rhoshirwaun and Sarn, we shall see on the left (within a mile of Aberdaron), on the slopes of Mynydd Ystum, another notable monument from the past. Castell Odo is an Iron Age hill-fort of the same type as those seen on Yr Eifl and Garn Fadryn. It is not as spectacular, but it is a good deal earlier, and is in fact the earliest relic of the Iron Age to be found in Wales. Pottery was discovered here some years ago which was of great value in enabling experts to date, not only this fortification, but also many others of the same type.

It is probable that what was originally seen at Castell Odo was a collection of wooden huts surrounded by a fence. This village, in common with many others, was certainly attacked and despoiled by invaders from the sea. And then, on the same site as the wooden encampment, a small, round, stone fort was constructed, and this is the structure that bears the name, Castell Odo.

Whereas the centre of Llŷn is wooded and

homely, with the Nanhoron Valley full of hazel trees all along its sheltered, winding length, the fields a lush green, and the primroses and bluebells a thick carpet in their season, the extreme end of Llŷn, as we saw when we approached Llangwnadl, is different. After climbing the steep hill out of Sarn, past the old farm of Meillteyrn on the right and into the parish of Bryncroes, we move into a locality which is much more barren and exposed. The fields are less protected, the houses are scattered, sometimes cursorily sheltered by one or two trees, all over the level heathland, and the wind carries the smell of the sea. There is something reminiscent of the West of Ireland here, from Pen-y-Groeslon to Rhoshirwaun. An occasional old farmhouse, perhaps as old as Bodwrdda, stands four-square against the weather, its grey stone buildings surrounded by a high wall.

In Aberdaron itself, Y Gegin Fawr has been here for ever, feeding pilgrims, sheltering them on beds of straw. It stands in the centre of the village, facing the Ship Inn, itself of respectable antiquity. But there was clearly a time when Y Gegin Fawr, together with the church of Saint Hywyn, was Aberdaron. It is a solid, square, whitewashed cottage, and the building that stands here now, apart from the slate roof, stood here in the fourteenth century when pilgrims finally made it down that hill and rested before going to look at the tossing sea, and the final obstacle of the tiderace.

But before thinking of crossing to Bardsey, it was necessary to go up to Uwchmynydd, to Capel

Mair and St Mary's Well, to give thanks for the journey so far completed, and to pray for a safe crossing. Up they would go, climbing the road we have not as yet explored, towards Uwchmynydd, which lies opposite the island of Bardsey, a high, exposed promontory three-and-a-half miles from Aberdaron.

On either side of the traveller, as he reaches the end of the road, and sees a solid track winding its way onwards and upwards, are two hills, Mynydd Mawr on the right, Mynydd Gwyddel on the left, and between them, on a green, fern-covered stretch of ground, where one can still see the shape of the foundations, they built Capel Mair. Rhabanian, that incorrigible romantic, brings it to life:

> It was built above a steep precipice on a patch of level ground, where it is claimed that every one of the gentry of Llŷn possessed some part of the plot of land on which it was built. The purpose of that old place of worship, which has now been listed these many years among the things of yesterday, was to receive pilgrims into the worship of their Redeemer, and to show hospitality to them in stormy weather, until they could finally cross to the old Insula Sanctorum of Bardsey . . .

I can never read Rhabanian's tight, black-bound little book without feeling the confident eccentricity of the man himself. For him, lost in a damp rectory at Llandudwen, the ancient beginnings of Llŷn were eccentrically alive. 'John Daniel, B.A.', he wrote in his book in 1892, and the copy I have was originally presented 'To Miss Lloyd Edwards,

With Very Best Wishes, From the Author'. The words are written in the blackest ink on the title page with a confident, flowery hand and Miss Lloyd Edwards, of course, is the daughter of Nanhoron. He begins a rambling introduction to the book with the words, 'No doubt there is nothing that gives a man greater pleasure than to come to know that which he was previously ignorant of'. An opening sentence worthy of Jane Austen.

Another tiny chapel, Capel Anelog, used to stand in the lee of the headland at one time, and they were both closely associated with Bardsey pilgrims. Past that green spot, a path leads downwards between the watching hills, directly towards the sea. The end of the journey is St Mary's Well. And we as children used to follow an old tradition regarding this well, perhaps the most famous of all the many sacred wells in Llŷn.

Having followed the path to the edge of the precipice where the sea boils and beats below, even on a calm and sunny day, and where Bardsey grows larger and larger on the horizon, the traveller will come to a set of stone stairs, carved out of the rock, leading down to the sea itself, where it washes the final steps, deep and green. He will have to look carefully to find the well at all. The sea waits, licking the broken rocks, and here, between land and sea, insignificant on its shelf, is the pilgrims' symbol of purity. It challenges the harshness of the sea in an apron of safety. Across a slimy green rock path that is constantly washed by waves, it is always still and clear. Myrddin describes it like this:

> The sea takes possession of it entirely at high tide. Nevertheless, as soon as the sea begins to ebb, its water, so powerful are its virtues, becomes completely clear again, with no trace of salt. A circuitous and dangerous path leads down to it, called Mary's Staircase . . .

The water is always pure. I can testify to that, many times over. The sea would pull at our feet as we crossed to it, leap up at us as we perched on our shelf. Then the superstition dictated that we should take a mouthful of water from the well. Then we had to run the sea's gauntlet back to the bottom of the steps and rapidly up the stone staircase until we stood clear above the well on a high rock, looking out to Bardsey. If the ancient travellers could do all that without swallowing the water, they would have a safe journey, they'd be blessed. For us, of course, it was a wishing well. Up there, looking out to sea at the humpback rock that was somehow so important, we held our breaths, and wished secret wishes, then ran excitedly away among the bracken and heather, mission completed.

On the way back, as we climbed the green path again, we passed Mynydd Gwyddel. It was a custom to send messages to Bardsey from this beacon hill whenever a body was on its way over to be buried. Such beacons flashed out through the dark all along the Celtic coasts, from Cornwall to Wester Ross, when invaders threatened from the sea; and they flickered across country from east to west to keep Llywelyn unscathed, and Glyndŵr. And they flashed out their messages of faith as well. And here they spoke of death.

Bardsey, as everyone knows, is the burial-ground of twenty thousand saints. We can assume that to be exaggeration, but it is certainly true that many Christians, in those early days, were carried long distances to be taken home to the holy ground of Bardsey. It was the nearest place to heaven. In the Cambrian Register for 1818, Ieuan Llŷn confidently lists those men of note who were buried there; the list includes Cadfan, Hywyn, Beuno, Padarn and Deiniol, among scores of others.

Saint Hywyn's church, in Aberdaron, stands at the edge of the sea. It's a simple, plain church, partly built during the twelfth century and extended during the fifteenth. It's obvious that during the rebuilding, the roof was considerably raised, as the east windows in the second nave are much higher than those in the original body of the church.

No one knows very much about Saint Hywyn, but it is assumed that he was one of that group that crossed over from Brittany, refugees from the barbarism of Europe at the beginning of the Dark Ages. Cadfan was another, and Maelrhys, and Aelrhiw, possibly, and many, of course, whose names have not survived. Whether Hywyn spent his time here or on Bardsey, there was a very close connection from the beginning between the church at Aberdaron and the priory on Bardsey. And Saint Hywyn's church became important in itself. It, like Clynnog and the cathedral church at Bangor, was a mother-church, and became a collegiate institution, with its complement of clergy. It also possessed the right of sanctuary; that is, the right to protect a fugitive from the secular authorities. And it is perhaps in connection with this right that the most famous story is told about Aberdaron church.

In the year 1115, when the running war between the princes of Wales and the Norman barons was at its height, Gwynedd was firmly in the grip of a great Welsh overlord, Gruffydd ap Cynan. But the south was a melting-pot, overrun, on the whole, by Normans. In fact, only one Welsh prince at that point was staging effective resistance to the Normans in the south, Gruffydd ap Rhys, the son of the eminent Rhys ap Tewdwr. Gruffydd ap Rhys was also Gruffydd ap Cynan's son-in-law, and he came up to Gwynedd to petition his father-in-law's support. Not only was the old fox unwilling to stretch his resources any further, he decided that he would consolidate his own position by giving his son-in-law into the hands of the English power. Gruffydd ap Rhys, discovering his intention, fled before him into Llŷn, and finally took refuge in the sanctuary church at Aberdaron. Contrary to all the traditions of chivalry, and indeed directly contrary to the Welsh laws of Hywel Dda, Gruffydd ap Cynan ordered that the sanctuary of the church should be violated, and Gruffydd ap Rhys taken. On hearing of this dishonourable intention, the clergy of Llŷn rose in protest. They came to Aberdaron in large numbers, and forced Gruffydd ap Cynan to change his mind. As a direct result of their intervention, Gruffydd ap Rhys was allowed to escape under cover of darkness and returned, no doubt a chastened man, to his own people at Ystrad Tywi.

The story, which is firmly based in scholarship, indicates that it was not easy for the secular power, whether Welsh or alien, to trespass on the territory of God's representatives in this part of the world. There is another story, much more apocryphal, which typifies, like the story of Maelrhys, the mixture of reality and fancy that rules here. As Myrddin has it:

> While the parishioners, one Sunday, were at their evening worship, pirates came from the sea and despoiled the church, in spite of all the efforts of the worshippers. But then the congregation turned to prayer, and while they were addressing the throne of grace, the despoilers returned to their ships, and at one stroke they and their ships sank into the depths of the sea.

It was always an ambition of mine as a boy to land on Bardsey. I knew nothing of saints and burial-places, but I always knew this island to be something special. I would sit by St Mary's Well and look at it, long to set foot on it, write poems, fey and fantastic about it. I would glimpse it at other times, from the wildness of Uwchmynydd in winter, the sea berserk on the rocks around the well, and think of it as a land of dreams.

Years later, when I actually stayed there, in a house set aside for retreat by the Church in Wales, I came to know it well. Brenda Chamberlain, the painter, was drawing to the end of her time there then, and there was still a permanent community on Bardsey, only a tiny remainder of the original hundred or more independent and often abrasive islanders who were here fifty years ago – but it was still a truly inhabited island. That community has now crossed to the mainland, Bardsey looks bereft, and landing on it last summer was a sad experience. The new Bardsey Island Trust has worked hard to bring life back to it again and there are summer dwellings and, of course, the bird observatory. But no real community. I stood on the rocks near Y Cafn, where boats have landed since the Dark Ages, and looked around. To the right, a grass track led past the farmhouses of Tŷ Pella and Cristin (where the Observatory has its headquarters), into the shadow of the mountain and on towards the northern extremity of the island, where a cluster of houses had gathered around a school and the chapel, and the ruins of the priory. A Lord Newborough gave the chapel to the inhabitants, and it is an utterly Victorian building, in its structure and in its furnishings and decoration, totally ill-suited in every way to the grey age of Bardsey. But useful, no doubt, to a living, worshipping community. And suited, at least, to their needs. The community, as it was early in the century, was much given to religious observance, very Sabbatical in its way of life, very much chapel-orientated, and the great Revivals came here in their turn. They used to hold eisteddfodau in the chapel as well, and hymn-singing festivals, and many would attend from the mainland, crossing in their best suits in the tossing boats.

As for the school, that, of course, was vital to the island's life. In fact, it was the departure of the school which was the death-knell of the true life of Bardsey in modern times. In the August 1932 number of a Welsh publication then extant, *Y Ford Gron*, there is an article by Olwen Eryri, where she writes of her seven years as a schoolteacher on Bardsey. She first crossed to the island in December, 1917, and in 1919, the Board of Education agreed to open an official school there. She ran it in the first instance for two years, and then left the island in the summer of 1921, when the population began to dwindle. But then, some years later, and this seems to have been the pattern over the centuries, the lure of Bardsey grew strong again, a number of the old inhabitants returned, together with many new faces, and the school was reopened. She writes of her two crossings, the one in 1917 and the other in January 1928. There must have been some perverse fate which caused one so trapped by the Bardsey legend to make her crossings at the worst possible time of the year, into a solitude of long, dark evenings and the howling wind. But she was certainly not deterred:

> It was in December 1917 that I crossed to Bardsey for the first time ever – not as a visitor, but with the intention of becoming an islander. This was during the era when rowing-boats were still being used, when it took between an hour and a half and two hours to complete the journey. It was at the time a novel experience for me to be at sea in an open boat in the depths of winter, and I was relieved to feel firm ground beneath my feet when I landed. My feelings were very mixed as I set foot on the island in the December dusk . . .

The second crossing was different. Bardsey had by now become a part of her, and there was no question of not returning, when she heard that the school was to reopen:

> . . . at the beginning of January, 1928, here we are again on Aberdaron beach, waiting for the boat to Bardsey – a motor-boat this time. It took us only three-quarters of an hour, and I was happy about that. New faces greeted me to Bardsey this time, but the nature of the welcome was the same . . . it was only the actual faces that had changed. Everything else was as it had always been – Y Cafn, where we landed, the mountain, the schoolhouse, the chapel, and the graves of the saints, all old friends. Life there was very similar to what it had been before. Although the island now possessed a strong motor-boat, you could still only cross the 'Swnt' when the sea was fairly calm and the wind favourable. At times we felt quite apart from the world . . .

The feeling of being quite apart from the world is the dominant feeling on Bardsey. One can sit on the slopes of Mynydd Enlli, and look over to Uwchmynydd and the piled-up hills of Llŷn, and consider oneself very far removed from the reality of anything that is happening beyond the limits of the island.

For this small strip of land, without question, has some special quality. Situated five miles to the south-west of the Llŷn peninsula, across a treacherous, sometimes deadly tiderace, it has created its own life. Its separateness and individual character are described in an official account, written during the nineteenth century:

> Bardsey: an island off the coast of Caernarfonshire about one and a half miles long and about a mile across. Its population in 1740 numbered 44 and in August 1798 there were 60 persons living in ten dwelling houses. It is outside the limits of any parish, and is exempt from tithes and rates . . . the produce of the island is cattle, sheep, potatoes, oats and barley.

The cattle were in fact taken over in a flat-bottomed boat, towed by a motor-boat, or, in the old days, by a rowing-boat, and it was only very recently indeed that any machinery at all arrived on the island. I have seen a calf transported in this way from Bardsey to Aberdaron; on a calm day, fortunately. Olwen Eryri, in the course of her account, speaks of the island's apartness:

> It was during the winter months that it was worst. After really stormy weather, the sea would be dangerous for weeks, and there would be no way of crossing to the mainland. And during those times we began to feel shortages. There was always a sufficiency of potatoes, and when things were really bad, we had more than enough of them, sometimes three meals a day. There was also an ample supply of milk, eggs, rabbits, apart, of course, from the constant store of salt fish. We always shared everything we had on an equal basis on these occasions, and always comforted each other with the certain conviction that fine weather must one day return . . .

It is still difficult to cross in winter, because The Sound, known originally as Ffrydlif Caswenan, not only has a fast tiderace running through it, but is also littered with rocks and whirlpools, and can be a most dangerous stretch of water, lethal to the unwary.

It isn't easy to assess the credibility of the various legends about the early days of Bardsey. So much has been written about it that the fact and legend have become inextricably intertwined, and one can only measure the volume of testimony in one direction or another. Everyone writes of Dubricius's connection with the island. He was an early saint, associated with south-east Wales, but certainly came to Bardsey to spend his last years. And he may well have been instrumental in building the priory. Most, however, link Cadfan and his band of Breton Christians with the building of an important Christian centre on Bardsey, and everyone also connects Bardsey, however loosely, with the monks of Bangor-on-Dee, who are said to have fled in all directions, many of them to Bardsey, when their own house was laid waste after the Battle of Chester in 615.

It is likely, however, that talk of Bardsey as a holy place was current long before Christian times, and that priests of ancient religions used it as a mystic centre of religious rites centuries before the Age of the Saints. This, once again, and perhaps supremely, shows us how the Christian pioneers were both superstitious and skilful enough to use sites already regarded as holy as the bases for their own missionary activity. They clearly needed to channel, rather than destroy, the strong loyalty to other religions, and the deep sense of the mystery of the universe, shown by the Celtic people. It is quite clear that Celtic Christianity incorporated many rites, customs and traditions from the Druidic culture, and that the patterns of worship, as well as the day to day rules, of the Celtic 'clas' would differ very substantially from the Norman customs that later came to Wales and superseded, at least on the surface, the old patterns of living and thinking. Gathering the evidence together, we can say with reasonable confidence, that a group of pioneering Christians, probably of the strongly militant, seafaring breed, came here some time in the middle of the sixth century, that they were all of the same tribe as that of Eneas the Breton, and that the names Cadfan and Hywyn can be attached to two of them.

We can also say that another notable pioneer, this time of Roman-Welsh extraction, Dubricius, came here in old age to meditate and to die, possibly before Cadfan and his crew arrived at all. It is also safe to assume that the monks of Bangor-on-Dee might well have looked on Bardsey, already famous for its sanctity, as a suitable place to seek peace and a resumption of community life after their corporate-trauma. What is equally certain is that from this point on, the sense of the island's sanctity and religious importance escalated to such an extent that it became legendary and unchallengeable. Giraldus Cambrensis wrote in 1188:

> Beyond Llŷn, there lies a small island where religious hermits, the Caelibes or Colidei, live. This island possesses, either because of the clemency of its climate, or because of some miracle and virtue of the saints, the remarkable characteristic, that the oldest there die first, as disease is infrequent, and hardly anyone ever dies, except as a result of great age . . .

And when Thomas Pennant crossed to the island, six centuries later, the same sense of awe and wonder prevailed:

> From the port of Aberdaron, I took boat for Bardsey Island, which lies about three leagues to the west. The mariners seemed tinctured with the piety of the place, for they had not rowed far, but they made a full stop, peeled off their hats, and offered up a short prayer. After doubling a head land, the island appears full in view; we passed under the lofty mountain which forms one side; after doubling the further end, we put into a little sandy creek, bounded by low rocks, as is the whole level part. On landing, I found all this tract a very fertile plain, well cultivated, and productive of everything which the island affords . . .

One gets an inaccurate impression of the geography and configuration of the island from the mainland. As several writers have mentioned, it seems squat, a hunchback rock, from Uwchmynydd, an outcrop of the same character, one might say, as Ynys Seiriol off Penmon. It is therefore something of a shock to see for the first time the green fields stretching away from the foot of the mountain towards the sea, both to the west and south, until they eventually peter out in the tattered rocks of the southern tip, where the lighthouse has now stood for a hundred years and more. In fact, Bardsey is about two miles long and about a mile and a half across, and most of that is rich, arable land, with the occasional farm hiding behind thick stone walls, and every structure built in the same clean grey stone, bleached by wind and rain.

After crossing Y Swnt, my boat did make its way along the south-eastern shore of the island, and then land, again as Pennant did, in the one sheltered inlet, Y Cafn, Bardsey's only landing-place.

And so I stood there, on the seaweed rocks of Y Cafn, and looked to the right, at the chapel and the cluster of houses, and to the left, at the lighthouse and the low-lying rocks. I remembered vividly how things had been twenty years before.

At that time, William Ifans lived in Tŷ Pella, the first farm one passes on the way to the remains of the priory, William and his wife and their son, Ernest. I used to cross to and fro in William's boat, and ever since he had decided to take up the tenancy of Tŷ Pella as a young man, although no sailor at the time, he had grown to be an expert boatman, as far as that particularly treacherous strip of sea was concerned. I still remember a journey with him during that period, and the way I recorded it in a journal I kept at the time:

> While we were in Aberdaron, the wind was strengthening all the time and I saw Ernest looking

dubiously at the sky more than once. And as we returned to Porth Meudwy, it was very obvious that the sea was far more stormy than it had been, and the sound of the wind whistling around the outer headland carried real menace. Even inshore, the boat was now heaving uneasily against the seaweed. I slipped and fell as I tried to gauge the right moment to jump in. It was only an indication of what was to come. After pulling out of the inlet, and hugging his way along the promontory towards the open channel, Wil began to express doubts whether we would be able to complete the journey at all. The boat was already rolling and bucking unsteadily and I could see the white horses were washing across Y Swnt. As soon as the bows cleared the shelter of the headland, the whole force of the gale hit us, and Wil had to keep his eyes on each oncoming wave and veer into it at the last minute to prevent it swamping the boat. Water was pouring in as it was, and I was completely soaked. I'd gone to sit in the bottom, with my back to the bows, nursing the faint hope that I might get less wet that way. I at least gained some shelter from the searing wind as I crouched as low as I could. It is, of course, quite irrational that one pins one's faith on a thin shell of boat against the whole monstrous strength of the sea. Nevertheless, a boat allied to the subtle handling of someone totally in command can be a sophisticated defence, if never an entirely convincing one. Wil Ifans keeps his boat on a knife-edge of control. Occasionally, he will switch off the motor and let the fragile shell ride some particular wave of its own volition, without the aggravating thrust of the engine. In the middle of it all, we lost the tiller. It slipped out of its sodden socket and bounced away among the smaller waves. Wil simply observed it, switched off the motor again, and executed a controlled drift towards it, sculling the boat with an oar over one side. Ultimately, he leaned over with the roll of a wave and scooped it calmly out of the foaming sea. There had scarcely been a change of expression on his face during all of this, but as he picked it out he allowed himself a transitory smile, firmly resetting his face at once as he tackled the wind again.

We were now out in the open sea, and for all I could experience around me we might have been a thousand miles from land. All I could see from my position below sea level was the heaving landscape of green waves, sometimes hurtling past and at other times overflowing on top of me, and forming a lazy pool around my feet. The depth of this I half-heartedly controlled with a tin mug. Often the wind threw the contents of the mug back in my face, but I was at least active, and combating the creeping cold. I wasn't actually feeling anything very much except an increasing anger every time the boat fell emptily into a gulley between two waves and shook my whole body with sickening regularity. I cursed helplessly as the boat shuddered against the unyielding water and as it rose on the next wave I gritted my teeth in expectation of the next descent.

If a film camera were to take a close-up of the journey, it would no doubt be exciting and full of tension, but inside it, the picture was simply cold, wet and infuriating. There was no sense of danger. You waited desperately for journey's end, not in order to reach safety, but in order to hurl away the wet clothes and know again what it was to be dry . . .

I still remember vividly the details of that journey, and I remember how certain was his command of the boat throughout. And I also remember how it felt after the journey was over:

> It's difficult to believe that this afternoon's journey happened at all, so brief was its excitement. The high tension of it has already slipped away into some memory-bank and I find it difficult to recall how my senses reacted at the time. I can still hear the great waves moving in on the far side of the island, and I feel a sudden warmth and sense of safety here in my own room. As I burrow in my sleeping-bag, snuff out the oil lamp and lie staring at the dying embers, the contrast between the plunging wooden boat and the solid, sea-beaten rock on which I'm lying now does begin to have some meaning. But it soon loses coherence as reality fades and the day ends . . .

Numerous times afterwards, I watched Wil Ifans's boat set off, from my perch high on the slopes of Mynydd Enlli, sometimes in a light cross wind, the waves running white and urgent in Y Swnt, at other times, often in the evening, when the sea was frozen still all the way across to the level horizon, and the phut-phut of his engine could be heard as clear as a bell over a mile and more. Brenda Chamberlain painted Wil and Ernest in that boat many times, and there's one painting in particular that stays in the mind, which shows the two slipping into Y Cafn in the evening light, with their long, sad faces, and the pink and grey and red of the painting re-creating an occasional quiet but threatening sunset after a windy day.

Beyond Tŷ Pella, also on the right, was the Bird Observatory. And Bardsey, of course, is famous as a stopping-place for migratory birds on their way south in the autumn, and on their way north in late spring. On the left, the track passes Carreg, where Brenda used to paint, and then much further on is Tŷ Isa, where Eddie and Jane lived. Jane is Wil's daughter, and Eddie is an Englishman caught up in the magic of islands. Having been both a sailor and a farm labourer, but with the island dream becoming more and more important in his mind, he came in the end to Bardsey, married Jane, and settled in Tŷ Isa, where the vegetables leapt from the soil all around him. As Olwen Eryri wrote, the community on Bardsey was always an entirely co-operative one. And it was still like that in the late nineteen-fifties. Everyone was involved in everything.

I remember a hay harvest in Eddie's fields. A hay harvest that took one back fifty years. A row of wooden rakes turning the hay to begin with, pitchforks raising and loading it onto carts, pitchforks again lifting it onto the rising stack in the barn. And tea in the open air, with Jane carrying it down to the field on a massive tray. And everyone taking part, bird-men, lighthouse-men, visitors like me, everyone.

Still further along the path, past the school, past the Victorian monument, set up in memory of the twenty thousand saints, stood Hendy, where I had my one room. From Hendy, you could hear the seals barking from the rocks below, and from there too you could see the rain and the gusts of wind rushing across the sea miles away before you felt their power beating at the walls of Hendy.

There was on Bardsey once, of course, a king. And that for purely practical reasons. Because Y Swnt was so often impassable, making the Bardsey community independent of the mainland for long stretches of time in winter, someone had to solve problems, make decisions, and sometimes mediate in disputes, on the island itself. So a leader would be elected, and that leader came to be called, no doubt facetiously to begin with, the King of Bardsey. But I think it was taken rather more seriously later. Lord Newborough made an imposing crown for the king, and the office carried no little prestige while there was a regular population of between fifty and a hundred permanently on Bardsey

So I looked at the island and walked back to the boat. Wil is dead now, but Ernest, married with a family, and Eddie and Jane and their ehildren, all still live in Uwchmynydd, a stone's throw from each other, and all within sight of the island that bred both Jane and Ernest. And they can be seen on Bardsey from time to time in summer.

On my way back to Aberdaron, I went around the southern tip, and straight across Y Swnt, it was so calm. The seals came to look at us, from a safe distance, and I could see Hendy looking out over the sea.

During the Middle Ages, when pilgrimage was a business, three pilgrimages to Bardsey were equal value to one pilgrimage to Rome. This was perhaps the most sacred place in the whole of Wales, and one of the most respected in Europe.

One anchorite, so they say, has made her home in two rooms in one of the empty farmhouses. She keeps a candle alight, on behalf of those who feel that there is a purpose in treasuring the long experience that has gone into some patches of earth. The past is still true. Bardsey is still, in some senses, the place where pilgrims can find their Holy Grail in a sense of inner peace. And that, I believe, was what growing up in Llŷn gave me. It is not a place which has given rise to great practical achievements. It is a place whose inhabitants are often hesitant and uncertain, faced with the more confident assertions of outsiders, but it has been a good place to hold in the mind, a small testimony to the ultimate sanity of the universe.